THE DARK CHILD

CAMARA LAYE

THE
DARK
CHILD

with an introduction by
PHILIPPE THOBY-MARCELLIN

FARRAR, STRAUS AND GIROUX   NEW YORK

To My Mother

Simple woman, patient woman, O mother, I think of you . . .

O Dâmon, Dâmon of the great race of blacksmiths, I think of you always; always you are with me, O Dâmon, my mother. How I should love to embrace you again, once again to be your child. . . .

Dark woman, African woman, O mother, I thank you for all you have done for me, your son, so far from you yet so near!

INTRODUCTION

The Dark Child, properly speaking, is not a novel. It is an autobiographical story to be read at one sitting, yet Camara Laye, with very simple means and without apparent art, manages to keep the reader in suspense until the end as in a work of pure fiction.

What gives it its charm, in my opinion, is the aura of dignity with which he has surrounded his family and his people as he paints them with candid sincerity, full of reserve and politeness, albeit without reticence. The measured frankness and tone of courteous modesty added to the authenticity of the testimonial catch one's attention from the very first lines.

I am afraid that those who would open this book with the thought of satisfying a hunger for the picturesque or escaping for a moment from the enervating condition of "civilized" man will be left unappeased. Unless they absolutely insist upon it, prejudice being stubborn, they will not find the classic "darkest Africa" nor the "prelogical mentality" so dear to the heart of the armchair traveler.

Of course, the book deals with animistic beliefs and practices, spirits intervene in the day-to-day life and a whole chapter is devoted to the rites of circumcision, but obviously the basis of the story is not to be found here. It is primarily universal man, man unqualified, with whom we are concerned. As a matter of fact, Camara Laye was born at Kouroussa in French Guinea, a country with an old civilization. He is descended from the black Sudanese who in the Middle Ages founded the fabulously rich Mali Empire which was ruled for six centuries by the Moslem dynasty of the Keytas.

If we are to believe the Arabian chroniclers of the time, the Malinké princes, who had about them theologians, scholars and musicians, carried on normal diplomatic relations and trade with the sovereigns of Morocco, Egypt and Portugal. "The caravans," Roger Vercel tells us, "would go down to the South, charged with salt, dates, figs, coral and textiles. They came back laden with ivory and ebony, rich with gold powder and ostrich feathers."

The most famous of the Mali Emperors, Kango Moussa, known as Moussa I, made a memorable pilgrimage to Mecca in 1324, with thirty kilos of precious powder and an impressive party of learned men, warriors and slaves, computed with characteristic oriental generosity as numbering between 8,000 and 60,000 persons. In Cairo, where they stopped on the journey to Mecca as well as on the journey back, the Sudanese made such extravagant purchases and gifts that the value of gold was affected—the miqtal fell from twenty-five to less than twenty-two drachmas.

But Kango Moussa did not frequent only the luxurious bazaars of Cairo. "The bookstores received his visit," Theodore Monod informs us, and when he returned to the Sudan, he brought back with him "a whole library of Canonical law." Besides, he was accompanied by a distinguished scholar whom he had met at Mecca, the Andalusian Abou Ichak el Gharnati, a poet and architect, who later built him palaces and mosques of rough-cast stone and acacia-wood frames, with crenellated terraces and pyramid-shaped minarets as well as an audience chamber in the Egyptian style, "decorated with brilliant arabesques."

Victim of the envy of neighboring states, the Mali Empire fell in the 18th century. Soon the Negroes of Upper Guinea like their brothers from the coast were subjected to the raids of the slave trade for the greater profit of the traders and planters of the New World. The French colonization came later. Thus a quick darkness fell over the history of this people, which has been dispelled to some extent by the Arabian chroniclers of the past. But the *griots*, those troubadours of black Africa, still recall to the Malinkés of today the deeds of their ancestors.

Frobenius has collected some of these legends (*African Genesis*, Stackpole Sons, New York, 1937). It is quite interesting to compare their style with that of *The Dark Child* and to find in them the same biblical sweep, the same parallelism and repetitions:

Four times Wagadu stood there in all her splendor. Four times Wagadu disappeared and was lost to human sight: once through vanity, once through falsehood, once through greed and once through dissension. Four times Wagadu changed her name. First she was called Dierra, then Agada, then Ganna, then Silla. Four times she turned her face. Once to the north, once to the west, once to the east and once to the south. For Wagadu, whenever men have seen her, has always had four gates: one to the north, one to the west, one to the east and one to the south. Those are the directions whence the strength of Wagadu comes, the strength in which she endures no matter whether she be built of stone, wood and earth or lives but as a shadow in the mind and longing of her children. For really, Wagadu is not of stone, not of wood, not of earth. Wagadu is the strength which lives in the hearts of men and is sometimes visible because eyes see her and ears hear the clash of swords and ring of shields, and is sometimes invisible because the indomitability of men has overtired her, so that she sleeps. Sleep came to Wagadu for the first time through vanity, for the second time through falsehood, for the third time through greed and for the fourth time through dissension. Should Wagadu ever be found for the fourth time, then she will live so forcefully in the minds of men that she will never be lost again, so forcefully that vanity, falsehood, greed and dissension will never be able to harm her.

—*Gassire's Lute*, pp. 97-98

Yet Camara Laye does not speak to us of his people's past. He makes neither direct reference nor the slightest allusion to it, and he is content to evoke for us with emotional restraint the simple life of a dark child of the great plain of Guinea—a story told at first hand, since it is his own; but an awareness of this past helps us better to understand the psychology of the author and his characters. For me, this past—veiled as in a watermark—is always associated with the story. And I see it clearly in such remarks as this:

> The woman's role in our country is one of fundamental independence, of great inner pride.

Or this other one:

> Perhaps we remained silent because of pride, or because of loyalty to the school. I know now that whatever the reason, it was stupid of us to keep silent. Such beatings were utterly alien to my people's passion for independence and equality.

I am also impressed by the frequent use of the word dignity or of its implicit presence when he speaks of those near to him and those whom he respects and consequently loves, as in this portrait of his mother:

> However, I am sure she walked away, as she always did, with great dignity. She had always held herself very erect, and that made her appear taller than she was.

I can not resist the temptation of applying to the whole Malinké people what he, an inhabitant of Kouroussa, tells us of the peasants of Tindican to whom he is so closely related:

I do not know how the idea of something rustic—I use the word in its accepted meaning: "lack of finesse, of delicacy"—became associated with country people. Civil formalities are more respected on the farm than in the city. Farm ceremony and manners are not understood by the city, which has no time for these things. To be sure, farm life is simpler than city life. But dealings between one man and another—perhaps because in the country everyone knows everyone else—are more strictly regulated. I used to notice a dignity everywhere which I have rarely found in cities. One did not act without duly considering such action, even though it were an entirely personal affair. The rights of others were highly respected. And if intelligence seemed slower it was because reflection preceded speech and because speech itself was a most serious matter.

These are cultural values that I feel should be emphasized, for I think that they have an interest at least equal to that of the superstitious practices to which the Malinkés still cling, despite their conversion to the Islamic religion, which already goes back about a thousand years. Throughout the world it is the primordial beliefs of mankind, particularly those of the popular religion, which are still the hardiest. Thus the pagan worship of heroes, to mention but one instance, fully survives in the Catholic worship of saints. This also explains the ease with which the slaves of Brazil, Cuba and San Domingo (now Haiti), who were forcibly christianized on landing, in turn identified the saints with the Negro deities.

The conversion of the Malinkés, however, did not bring about the same syncretism. The Moslem religion was simply superimposed on the old African animism, discarding of course the principal gods to the advantage of Allah, while allowing the secondary spirits to survive just as they were. But fundamentally the difference is not important.

If it is true that animistic beliefs are general in Upper Guinea ("popular," in fact), there is nevertheless an élite which does not share them—men such as Camara Laye and his uncle Mamadou, who studies Arabian by himself so that he can better attune his conduct to the precepts of the Koran.

But we are far afield from the intentions of the author, who wanted to tell his own story and touch the reader. We must admit that he has succeeded and that the book has the force of the nostalgia which spurred him to write it to relieve his exile at a time when he was far from his people. We are eager to know the rest—his life as a poor student in Paris, and most of all the return to his native land.

PHILIPPE THOBY-MARCELIN

Translated from the French by Eva Thoby-Marcelin

THE DARK CHILD

I was a little boy playing around my father's hut. How old would I have been at that time? I can not remember exactly. I must still have been very young: five, maybe six years old. My mother was in the workshop with my father, and I could just hear their familiar voices above the noise of the anvil and the conversation of the customers.

Suddenly I stopped playing, my whole attention fixed on a snake that was creeping around the hut. After a moment I went over to him. I had taken in my hand a reed that was lying in the yard—there were always some lying around; they used to get broken off the fence of plaited reeds that marked the boundary of our concession—and I thrust it into his mouth. The snake did not try to get away: he was beginning to enjoy our little game; he was slowly swallowing the reed; he was devouring it, I thought, as if it were some delicious prey, his eyes glittering with voluptuous bliss; and inch by inch his head was drawing nearer to my hand. At last the reed was almost entirely swallowed, and the snake's jaws were terribly close to my fingers.

I was laughing. I had not the slightest fear, and I feel sure that the snake would not have hesitated much longer before burying his fangs in my fingers if, at that moment, Damany, one of the apprentices, had not come out of the workshop. He called my father, and almost at once I felt myself lifted off my feet: I was safe in the arms of one of my father's friends.

Around me there was a great commotion. My mother was shouting hardest of all, and she gave me a few sharp slaps. I wept, more upset by the sudden uproar than by the blows. A little later, when I was somewhat calmer and the shouting had ceased, my mother solemnly warned me never to play that game again. I promised, although the game still didn't seem dangerous to me.

My father's hut was near the workshop, and I often played beneath the veranda that ran around the outside. It was his private hut, and like all our huts built of mud bricks that had been pounded and moulded with water; it was round, and proudly helmeted with thatch. It was entered by a rectangular doorway. Inside, a tiny window let in a thin shaft of daylight. On the right was the bed, made of beaten earth like the bricks, and spread with a simple wicker-work mat on which lay a pillow stuffed with kapok. At the rear, right under the window where the light was strongest, were the tool-boxes. On the left were the *boubous* and the prayer-rugs. At the head of the bed, hanging over the pillow and watching over my father's slumber, stood a row of pots that contained extracts from plants and the bark of trees. These pots all had metal lids and were profusely and curiously garlanded with chaplets of cowry shells; it did not take me long to discover that they were the most important things in the hut; they contained magic charms—those mysterious liquids that keep the evil spirits at bay, and, if smeared on the body, make it invulnerable to every kind of black magic. My father, before going to bed, never failed to smear his body with a little of each liquid, first one, then another, for each charm had its own particular property: but exactly *what* property I did not know: I had left my father's house too soon.

From the veranda under which I played I could keep an eye on the workshop opposite, and the adults for their part could keep an eye on me. This workshop was the main building in our concession, and my father was generally to be found there, looking after the work, forging the most important items himself, or repairing delicate mechanisms; there he received his friends and his customers, and the place resounded with noise from morning to night. Moreover, everyone who entered or left our concession had to cross the workshop. There was a perpetual coming and going, though no one seemed to be in any particular hurry; each had his bit of gossip; each lingered at the forge to watch. Sometimes I came near the door, but I rarely went in; everyone there frightened me, and I would run away as soon as anyone tried to touch me. It was not until very much later that I got into the habit of crouching in a corner of the workshop to watch the fire blazing in the forge.

My private domain at that time was the veranda that encircled my father's hut, my mother's hut, and the orange tree that grew in the middle of the concession.

As soon as you crossed the workshop and went through the door at the back, you would see the orange tree. Compared with the giants of our native forests, the tree was not very big, but its mass of glossy leaves cast a dense shade that kept the heat at bay. When it was in flower a heady perfume pervaded the entire concession. When the fruit first appeared we were only allowed to look: we had to wait patiently until it was ripe. Then my father, who as head of the family—and a very large family it was—governed the concession, gave the order to pick the fruit. The men who did the picking brought their baskets one by one to my father, who portioned them out among the people who lived in the concession and among his neighbors and customers. After that we were permitted to help ourselves from the baskets and we were allowed as much as we liked! My father was open-handed; in fact, a lavish giver. Any visitor, no matter who he was, shared our meals; since I could never keep up with the speed at which such guests ate I might have remained forever hungry if my mother had not taken the precaution of putting my share aside.

"Sit here," she would say, "and eat, for your father's mad."

She did not look upon such guests with a kindly eye. There were too many for her liking, all bent on filling their bellies at her expense. My father, for his part, ate very little; he was an extremely temperate man.

We lived beside a railroad. The trains skirted the reed fence of the concession so closely that sparks thrown off from the locomotive set fire to it every now and then which had to be quickly extinguished so that the whole concession would not go up in smoke. These alarms, frightening yet exciting, made me aware of the passing trains. And even where there were no trains—for in those days the railroad was dependent on a most irregular water traffic—much of my time was spent watching the iron rails. They glistened cruelly in a light which nothing in that place could relieve. Baking since dawn, the roadbed was so hot that oil which dropped from the locomotives evaporated immediately, leaving no trace. Was it the oven-like heat or the smell of oil—for the smell remained in spite of everything—which attracted the snakes? I do not know. But often I came upon them crawling in that hot road-bed. It would have been fatal if they had gotten into the concession.

Ever since the day when I had been forbidden by my mother to play with snakes I ran to her as soon as I saw one.

"There's a snake!" I would cry.

"What? Another?"

And she would come running to see what sort of snake it was. If it was just a snake like any other snake—actually they were all quite different—she would immediately beat it to death; and, like all the women of our country, she would work herself into a frenzy, beating the snake to a pulp. The men contented themselves with a single hard blow, neatly struck.

One day, however, I noticed a little black snake with a strikingly marked body. He was proceeding slowly in the direction of the workshop. I ran to warn my mother, as usual. But as soon as she saw the black snake she said to me gravely:

"My son, this one must not be killed: he is not like other snakes, and he will not harm you; you must never interfere with him."

Everyone in our concession knew that this snake must not be killed—everyone except myself, and, I suppose, my little playmates, who were still ignorant children.

"This snake," my mother added, "is your father's guiding spirit."

I gazed dumbfounded at the little snake. He was proceeding calmly toward the workshop, gracefully, very sure of himself, and almost as if conscious of his immunity; his body, black and brilliant, glittered in the harsh light of the sun. When he reached the workshop, I noticed for the first time a small hole in the wall, cut out level with the ground. The snake disappeared through this hole.

"Look," said my mother, "the snake is going to pay your father a visit."

Although I was familiar with the supernatural, this sight filled me with such astonishment that I was struck dumb. What business would a snake have with my father? And why this particular snake? No one was to kill him because he was my father's guiding spirit! At any rate, that was the explanation my mother had given me. But what exactly *was* a "guiding spirit"? What were these guiding spirits that I encountered almost everywhere, forbidding one thing, commanding another to be done? I could not understand it at all, though their presences surrounded me as I grew to manhood. There were good spirits, and there were evil ones; and more evil than good ones, it seemed. And how was I to know that this snake was harmless? He was a snake like the others: black, to be sure, with extraordinary markings—but for all that a snake. I was completely perplexed, but I did not question my mother: I had decided that I must ask my father about it, as if this were a mystery to be discussed only between men, a mystery in which women had no part. I decided to wait until evening to speak to him.

Immediately after the evening meal, when the palavers were over, my father bade his friends farewell and sat under the veranda of his hut; I seated myself near him. I began questioning him in a dilatory manner, as all children do, regarding every subject under the sun. Actually I was no more talkative than on other evenings. Only this evening I withheld what troubled me, waiting for the opportunity when— my face betraying nothing—I might ask the question which had worried me so deeply from the moment when I first saw the black snake going toward the workshop. Finally, unable to restrain myself any longer, I asked:

"My father, what is that little snake that comes to visit you?"

"What snake do you mean?"

"Why, the little black snake that my mother forbids us to kill."

"Ah!" he said.

He gazed at me for a long while. He seemed to be considering whether to answer or not. Perhaps he was thinking about how old I was, perhaps he was wondering if it was not a little too soon to confide such a secret to a twelve-year-old boy. Then suddenly he made up his mind.

"That snake," he said, "is the guiding spirit of our race. Can you understand that?"

"Yes," I answered, although I did not understand very well.

"That snake," he went on, "has always been with us; he has always made himself known to one of us. In our time, it is to me that he has made himself known."

"Yes," I said.

And I said it with all my heart, for it seemed obvious to me that the snake could have made himself known to no one but my father. Was not my father the head man in our concession? Was it not my father who had authority over all the blacksmiths in our district? Was he not the most skilled? Was he not, after all, my father?

"How did he make himself known?" I asked.

"First of all, he made himself known in the semblance of a dream. He appeared to me several times in sleep and told me the day on which he would appear to me in reality: he gave me the precise time and place. But when I really saw him for the first time, I was filled with fear. I took him for a snake like any other snake, and I had to keep myself under control or I would have tried to kill him. When he saw that I did not receive him kindly, he turned away and departed the way he had come. And there I stood, watching him depart, wondering all the time if I should not simply have killed him there and then; but a power greater than I stayed my hand and prevented me from pursuing him. I stood watching him disappear. And even then, at that very moment, I could easily have overtaken him; a few swift strides would have been enough; but I was struck motionless by a kind of paralysis. Such was my first encounter with the little black snake."

He was silent a moment, then went on:

"The following night, I saw the snake again in my dream. 'I came as I foretold,' he said, 'but thou didst not receive me kindly; nay, rather I did perceive that thou didst intend to receive me unkindly: I did read it thus in thine eyes. Wherefore dost thou reject me? Lo, I am the guiding spirit of thy race, and it is even as the guiding spirit of thy race that I make myself known to thee, as to the most worthy. Therefore forbear to look with fear upon me, and beware that thou dost not reject me, for behold, I bring thee good fortune.' After that, I received the snake kindly when he made himself known to me a second time; I received him without fear, I received him with loving kindness, and he brought me nothing but good."

My father again was silent for a moment, then he said: "You can see for yourself that I am not more gifted than other men, that I have nothing which other men have not also, and even that I have less than others, since I give everything away, and would even give away the last thing I had, the shirt on my back. Nevertheless I am better known. My name is on everyone's tongue, and it is I who have authority over all the blacksmiths in the five cantons. If these things are so, it is by virtue of this snake alone, who is the guiding spirit of our race. It is to this snake that I owe everything; it is he who gives me warning of all that is to happen. Thus I am never surprised, when I awake, to see this or that person waiting for me outside my workshop: I already know that he will be there. No more am I surprised when this or that motorcycle or bicycle breaks down, or when an accident happens to a clock: because I have had foreknowledge of what would come to pass. Everything is transmitted to me in the course of the night, together with an account of all the work I shall have to perform, so that from the start, without having to cast about in my mind, I know how to repair whatever is brought to me. These things have established my renown as a craftsman. But all this—let it never be forgotten —I owe to the snake, I owe it to the guiding spirit of our race."

He was silent; and then I understood why, when my father came back from a walk he would enter the workshop and say to the apprentices: "During my absence, this or that person has been here, he was dressed in such and such a way, he came from such and such a place and he brought with him such and such a piece of work to be done." And all marveled at this curious knowledge. When I raised my eyes, I saw that my father was watching me.

"I have told you all these things, little one, because you are my son, the eldest of my sons, and because I have nothing to hide from you. There is a certain form of behavior to observe, and certain ways of acting in order that the guiding spirit of our race may approach you also. I, your father, was observing that form of behavior which persuades our guiding spirit to visit us. Oh, perhaps not consciously: but nevertheless it is true that if you desire the guiding spirit of our race to visit you one day, if you desire to inherit it in your turn, you will have to conduct yourself in the selfsame manner; from now on, it will be necessary for you to be more and more in my company."

He gazed at me with burning eyes, then suddenly he heaved a sigh.

"I fear, I very much fear, little one, that you are not often enough in my company. You are all day at school, and one day you will depart from that school for a greater one. You will leave me, little one. . . ."

And again he heaved a sigh. I saw that his heart was heavy within him. The hurricane-lamp hanging on the veranda cast a harsh glare on his face. He suddenly seemed to me an old man.

"Father!" I cried.

"Son . . ." he whispered.

And I was no longer sure whether I ought to continue to attend school or whether I ought to remain in the workshop: I felt unutterably confused.

"Go now," said my father.

I went to my mother's hut. The night was full of sparkling stars; an owl was hooting nearby. Ah! what was the right path for me? Did I know yet where that path lay? My perplexity was boundless as the sky, and mine was a sky, alas, without any stars. . . . I entered my mother's hut, which at that time was mine also, and went to bed at once. But sleep did not come and I tossed restlessly on my bed.

"What's the matter with you?" asked my mother.

"Nothing."

No. I couldn't find anything to say.

"Why don't you go to sleep?" my mother continued.

"I don't know."

"Go to sleep!" she said.

"Yes," I said.

"Sleep . . . Nothing can resist sleep," she said sadly.

Why did she, too, appear so sad? Had she divined my distress? Anything that concerned me she sensed very deeply. I was trying to sleep, but I shut my eyes and lay still in vain: the image of my father under the hurricane-lamp would not leave me: my father who had suddenly seemed so old and who was so young, so lively—younger and livelier than the rest of us, a man no one could outrun, who was swifter of limb than any of us. . . . "Father! . . . Father! . . . !" I kept repeating. "What must I do if I am to do the right thing?" And I wept silently and fell asleep still weeping.

After that we never mentioned the little black snake again: my father had spoken to me about him for the first and last time. But from that time on, as soon as I saw the little snake, I would run and sit in the workshop. I would watch him glide through the little hole in the wall. As if informed of his presence, my father at that very instant would turn his eyes to the hole and smile. The snake would go straight to him, opening his jaws. When he was within reach my father would stroke him and the snake would accept the caress with a quivering of his whole body. I never saw the little snake attempt to do the slightest harm to my father. That caress and the answering tremor—but I ought to say: that appealing caress and that answering tremor—threw me each time into an inexpressible confusion. I imagined I know not what mysterious conversations: the hand inquired and the tremor replied. . . .

Yes. It was like a conversation. Would I too converse that way some day? No. I would continue to attend school. Yet I should have liked so much to place my hand, my own hand, on that snake, and to understand and listen to that tremor too; but I did not know whether the snake would have accepted my hand, and I felt now that he would have nothing to tell me. I was afraid that he would never have anything to tell me.

When my father felt that he had stroked the snake enough he left him alone. Then the snake coiled himself under the edge of one of the sheepskins on which my father, facing his anvil, was seated.

Of all the different kinds of work my father engaged in, none fascinated me so much as his skill with gold. No other occupation was so noble, no other needed such a delicate touch. And then, every time he worked in gold it was like a festival —indeed it *was* a festival—that broke the monotony of ordinary working days.

So, if a woman, accompanied by a go-between, crossed the threshold of the workshop, I followed her in at once. I knew what she wanted: she had brought some gold, and had come to ask my father to transform it into a trinket. She had collected it in the placers of Siguiri where, crouching over the river for months on end, she had patiently extracted grains of gold from the mud.

These women never came alone. They knew my father had other things to do than make trinkets. And even when he had the time, they knew they were not the first to ask a favor of him, and that, consequently, they would not be served before others.

Generally they required the trinket for a certain date, for the festival of Ramadan or the Tabaski or some other family ceremony or dance.

Therefore, to enhance their chances of being served quickly and to more easily persuade my father to interrupt the work before him, they used to request the services of an official praise-singer, a go-between, arranging in advance the fee they were to pay him for his good offices.

The go-between installed himself in the workshop, tuned up his *cora*, which is our harp, and began to sing my father's praises. This was always a great event for me. I heard recalled the lofty deeds of my father's ancestors and their names from the earliest times. As the couplets were reeled off it was like watching the growth of a great genealogical tree that spread its branches far and wide and flourished its boughs and twigs before my mind's eye. The harp played an accompaniment to this vast utterance of names, expanding it with notes that were now soft, now shrill.

I could sense my father's vanity being inflamed, and I already knew that after having sipped this milk-and-honey he would lend a favorable ear to the woman's request. But I was not alone in my knowledge. The woman also had seen my father's eyes gleaming with contented pride. She held out

her grains of gold as if the whole matter were settled. My
father took up his scales and weighed the gold.

"What sort of trinket do you want?" he would ask.

"I want. . . ."

And then the woman would not know any longer exactly
what she wanted because desire kept making her change her
mind, and because she would have liked all the trinkets at
once. But it would have taken a pile of gold much larger
than she had brought to satisfy her whim, and from then on
her chief purpose in life was to get hold of it as soon as she
could.

"When do you want it?"

Always the answer was that the trinket was needed for an
occasion in the near future.

"So! You are in that much of a hurry? Where do you think
I shall find the time?"

"I am in a great hurry, I assure you."

"I have never seen a woman eager to deck herself out who
wasn't in a great hurry! Good! I shall arrange my time to
suit you. Are you satisfied?"

He would take the clay pot that was kept specially for
smelting gold, and would pour the grains into it. He would
then cover the gold with powdered charcoal, a charcoal he
prepared by using plant juices of exceptional purity. Finally,
he would place a large lump of the same kind of charcoal
over the pot.

As soon as she saw that the work had been duly under-
taken, the woman, now quite satisfied, would return to her
household tasks, leaving her go-between to carry on with the
praise-singing which had already proved so advantageous.

At a sign from my father the apprentices began working two sheepskin bellows. The skins were on the floor, on opposite sides of the forge, connected to it by earthen pipes. While the work was in progress the apprentices sat in front of the bellows with crossed legs. That is, the younger of the two sat, for the elder was sometimes allowed to assist. But the younger —this time it was Sidafa—was only permitted to work the bellows and watch while waiting his turn for promotion to less rudimentary tasks. First one and then the other worked hard at the bellows: the flame in the forge rose higher and became a living thing, a genie implacable and full of life.

Then my father lifted the clay pot with his long tongs and placed it on the flame.

Immediately all activity in the workshop almost came to a halt. During the whole time that the gold was being smelted, neither copper nor aluminum could be worked nearby, lest some particle of these base metals fall into the container which held the gold. Only steel could be worked on such occasions, but the men, whose task that was, hurried to finish what they were doing, or left it abruptly to join the apprentices gathered around the forge. There were so many, and they crowded so around my father, that I, the smallest person present, had to come near the forge in order not to lose track of what was going on.

If he felt he had inadequate working space, my father had the apprentices stand well away from him. He merely raised his hand in a simple gesture: at that particular moment he never uttered a word, and no one else would: no one was allowed to utter a word. Even the go-between's voice was no longer raised in song. The silence was broken only by the panting of the bellows and the faint hissing of the gold. But if my father never actually spoke, I know that he was forming words in his mind. I could tell from his lips, which kept moving, while, bending over the pot, he stirred the gold and charcoal with a bit of wood that kept bursting into flame and had constantly to be replaced by a fresh one.

What words did my father utter? I do not know. At least I am not certain what they were. No one ever told me. But could they have been anything but incantations? On these occasions was he not invoking the genies of fire and gold, of fire and wind, of wind blown by the blast-pipes of the forge, of fire born of wind, of gold married to fire? Was it not their assistance, their friendship, their espousal that he besought? Yes. Almost certainly he was invoking these genies, all of whom are equally indispensable for smelting gold.

The operation going on before my eyes was certainly the smelting of gold, yet something more than that: a magical operation that the guiding spirits could regard with favor or disfavor. That is why, all around my father, there was absolute silence and anxious expectancy. Though only a child, I knew there could be no craft greater than the goldsmith's. I expected a ceremony; I had come to be present at a ceremony; and it actually was one, though very protracted. I was still too young to understand why, but I had an inkling as I watched the almost religious concentration of those who followed the mixing process in the clay pot.

When finally the gold began to melt I could have shouted aloud—and perhaps we all would have if we had not been forbidden to make a sound. I trembled, and so did everyone else watching my father stir the mixture—it was still a heavy paste—in which the charcoal was gradually consumed. The next stage followed swiftly. The gold now had the fluidity of water. The genies had smiled on the operation!

"Bring me the brick!" my father would order, thus lifting the ban that until then had silenced us.

The brick, which an apprentice would place beside the fire, was hollowed out, generously greased with Galam butter. My father would take the pot off the fire and tilt it carefully, while I would watch the gold flow into the brick, flow like liquid fire. True, it was only a very sparse trickle of fire, but how vivid, how brilliant! As the gold flowed into the brick, the grease sputtered and flamed and emitted a thick smoke that caught in the throat and stung the eyes, leaving us all weeping and coughing.

But there were times when it seemed to me that my father ought to turn this task over to one of his assistants. They were experienced, had assisted him hundreds of times, and could certainly have performed the work well. But my father's lips moved and those inaudible, secret words, those incantations he addressed to one we could not see or hear, was the essential part. Calling on the genies of fire, of wind, of gold and exorcising the evil spirits—this was a knowledge he alone possessed.

By now the gold had been cooled in the hollow of the brick, and my father began to hammer and stretch it. This was the moment when his work as a goldsmith really began. I noticed that before embarking on it he never failed to stroke the little snake stealthily as it lay coiled up under the sheepskin. I can only assume that this was his way of gathering strength for what remained to be done, the most trying part of his task.

But was it not extraordinary and miraculous that on these occasions the little black snake was always coiled under the sheepskin? He was not always there. He did not visit my father every day. But he was always present whenever there was gold to be worked. His presence was no surprise to *me*. After that evening when my father had spoken of the guiding spirit of his race I was no longer astonished. The snake was there intentionally. He knew what the future held. Did he tell my father? I think that he most certainly did. Did he tell him everything? I have another reason for believing firmly that he did.

The craftsman who works in gold must first of all purify himself. That is, he must wash himself all over and, of course, abstain from all sexual commerce during the whole time. Great respecter of ceremony as he was, it would have been impossible for my father to ignore these rules. Now, I never saw him make these preparations. I saw him address himself to his work without any apparent preliminaries. From that moment it was obvious that, forewarned in a dream by his black guiding spirit of the task which awaited him in the morning, my father must have prepared for it as soon as he arose, entering his workshop in a state of purity, his body smeared with the secret potions hidden in his numerous pots of magical substances; or perhaps he always came into his workshop in a state of ritual purity. I am not trying to make him out a better man than he was—he was a man and had his share of human frailties—but he was always uncompromising in his respect for ritual observance.

The woman for whom the trinket was being made, and who had come often to see how the work was progressing, would arrive for the final time, not wanting to miss a moment of this spectacle—as marvelous to her as to us—when the gold wire, which my father had succeeded in drawing out from the mass of molten gold and charcoal, was transformed into a trinket.

There she would be. Her eyes would devour the fragile gold wire, following it in its tranquil and regular spiral around the little slab of metal which supported it. My father would catch a glimpse of her and I would see him slowly beginning to smile. Her avid attention delighted him.

"Are you trembling?" he would ask.

"Am I trembling?"

And we would all burst out laughing at her. For she would be trembling! She would be trembling with covetousness for the spiral pyramid in which my father would be inserting, among the convolutions, tiny grains of gold. When he had finally finished by crowning the pyramid with a heavier grain, she would dance in delight.

No one—no one at all—would be more enchanted than she as my father slowly turned the trinket back and forth between his fingers to display its perfection. Not even the praise-singer whose business it was to register excitement would be more excited than she. Throughout this metamorphosis he did not stop speaking faster and ever faster, increasing his tempo, accelerating his praises and flatteries as the trinket took shape, shouting to the skies my father's skill.

For the praise-singer took a curious part—I should say rather that it was direct and effective—in the work. He was drunk with the joy of creation. He shouted aloud in joy. He plucked his *cora* like a man inspired. He sweated as if he were the trinket-maker, as if he were my father, as if the trinket were his creation. He was no longer a hired censer-bearer, a man whose services anyone could rent. He was a man who created his song out of some deep inner necessity. And when my father, after having soldered the large grain of gold that crowned the summit, held out his work to be admired, the praise-singer would no longer be able to contain himself. He would begin to intone the *douga*, the great chant which is sung only for celebrated men and which is danced for them alone.

But the *douga* is a formidable chant, a provocative chant, a chant which the praise-singer dared not sing, and which the man for whom it is sung dared not dance before certain precautions had been taken. My father had taken them as soon as he woke, since he had been warned in a dream. The praise-singer had taken them when he concluded his arrangements with the woman. Like my father he had smeared his body with magic substances and had made himself invulnerable to the evil genies whom the *douga* inevitably set free; these potions made him invulnerable also to rival praise-singers, perhaps jealous of him, who awaited only this song and the exaltation and loss of control which attended it, in order to begin casting their spells.

At the first notes of the *douga* my father would arise and emit a cry in which happiness and triumph were equally mingled; and brandishing in his right hand the hammer that was the symbol of his profession and in his left a ram's horn filled with magic substances, he would dance the glorious dance.

No sooner had he finished, than workmen and apprentices, friends and customers in their turn, not forgetting the woman for whom the trinket had been created, would flock around him, congratulating him, showering praises on him and complimenting the praise-singer at the same time. The latter found himself laden with gifts—almost his only means of support, for the praise-singer leads a wandering life after the fashion of the troubadours of old. Aglow with dancing and the praises he had received, my father would offer everyone cola nuts, that small change of Guinean courtesy.

Now all that remained to be done was to redden the trinket in a little water to which chlorine and sea salt had been added. I was at liberty to leave. The festival was over! But often as I came out of the workshop my mother would be in the court, pounding millet or rice, and she would call to me:

"Where have you been?" although she knew perfectly well where I had been.

"In the workshop."

"Of course. Your father was smelting gold. Gold! Always gold!"

And she would beat the millet or rice furiously with her pestle.

"Your father is ruining his health!"

"He danced the *douga*."

"The *douga*! The *douga* won't keep him from ruining his eyes. As for you, you would be better off playing in the court-yard instead of breathing dust and smoke in the workshop."

My mother did not like my father to work in gold. She knew how dangerous it was: a trinket-maker empties his lungs blowing on the blow-pipe and his eyes suffer from the fire. Perhaps they suffer even more from the microscopic precision which the work requires. And even if there had been no such objections involved, my mother would scarcely have relished this work. She was suspicious of it, for gold can not be smelted without the use of other metals, and my mother thought it was not entirely honest to put aside for one's own use the gold which the alloy had displaced. However, this was a custom generally known, and one which she herself had accepted when she took cotton to be woven and received back only a piece of cotton cloth half the weight of the original bundle.

THREE

I often spent a few days at Tindican, a tiny village west of Kouroussa where my mother had been born, and where her mother and brothers still lived. Since they were very fond of me, I was always delighted to visit them. They pampered me, especially my grandmother who made a festive occasion of my arrival. As for me, I loved her with all my heart.

She was a large woman, slender, erect, and robust. Her hair remained black as long as I knew her. Actually she was still young and had not given up farming although her sons, who were able-bodied men, tried to dissuade her from it. She disliked idleness and the secret of her youth no doubt lay in constant activity. Her husband had died young, far too young. I never saw him. Sometimes she would talk to me about him, but never for very long. Tears soon interrupted her account, and I never learned anything about my grandfather, anything which might have given me a sense of the sort of person he had been—for my mother and my uncles did not talk about him either. In my country, the dead who have been much loved are hardly mentioned at all; we are too distressed when evoking such memories.

When I went to Tindican, my youngest uncle came to fetch me. Younger than my mother, he seemed nearer my age than hers. He was good by nature, and there was no need for her to remind him to keep an eye on me; he did so of his own accord. Since I was only a child, he would shorten his steps to suit my pace. He did this so effectively that we made the usual two hours' walk to Tindican in four. But I was hardly aware of the length of the road, for all sorts of marvels lay along it.

I say "marvels," for Kouroussa is actually a city and hasn't any of those country sights which a city child always finds marvelous. As we walked along we were likely to dislodge a hare or a wild boar; birds flew away at our approach, with a great beating of wings; sometimes we would meet a crowd of monkeys. Every time something like this happened I felt a small thrill of excitement, for I was more startled than the game which had been suddenly alerted. Observing my pleasure, my uncle would throw a fistful of pebbles a long way ahead; or he would beat the tall grass with a dead branch, to dislodge birds and animals. I would imitate him, but never for very long. The afternoon sun beat fiercely on the savannah, and I would return to slip my hand into his. Once again we would go along quietly.

"Aren't you getting too tired?" he would ask.

"No."

"We could rest a bit if you'd like."

He would choose a kapok tree whose shade he thought sufficiently dense, and we would sit down. He would tell me the most recent news from the farm: which cow had calved, and which had just been bought; which field had been plowed and what damage the wild boars had done. The new-born calves interested me the most.

"We have a new calf," he would say.

"Whose?" I would ask, for I knew each beast in the herd.

"The white cow's."

"The one with horns like a crescent moon?"

"Yes."

"Ah! And the calf. How is it?"

"Beautiful! Beautiful! It has a white star on its forehead."

"A star?"

"Yes. A star."

I would daydream a bit over this star. A calf with a star. It should become the leader of the herd.

"It must be very beautiful."

"You couldn't dream of anything more beautiful. Its ears are so rosy you'd think they were transparent."

"I want to see it. Will we, when we get there?"

"Of course."

"You'll come with me to see it?"

"Of course. Chicken heart!"

For I was afraid of the great horned beasts. My playmates

at Tindican were perfectly at ease with them in all sorts of ways. These children were not afraid to jump on the backs or hang from the horns of the animals. When I drove the cattle into the bush, I would watch them graze from a distance, but never came too close. I liked them, but their horns frightened me. To be sure, the calves did not have horns, but their movements were abrupt and unexpected, and one could not depend on them to stay in one place.

"Let's go on," I would say. "We've rested enough."

I was always in a hurry to get there. If the calf was in the corral I could pet it, for there the animals were quiet. I would put a little salt on the palm of my hand for the calf to lick. Its tongue gently grated on my hand.

"Let's go," I would say again.

But my legs were too short for speed; my pace would slacken, and we would saunter along. Then it was that my uncle told me how the monkey had tricked the panther who was all ready to eat him, how the palm tree rat had kept the hyena waiting all night for nothing. These were stories I had already heard a hundred times, but I always enjoyed them and laughed so loudly that the wild fowl ahead of us took flight.

Before we had actually arrived at Tindican we would meet my grandmother who always came to greet us. I would slip my hand out of my uncle's and run toward her, shouting. She would pick me up and embrace me, and I embraced her in return, overcome with joy.

"How is my little husband getting on?" she would ask.

"Fine. Fine."

"Is that really so?"

And she would look at me and touch me to see if my cheeks were full and if I had anything but skin on my bones. If the examination satisfied her she congratulated me. If not —for growing had made me thin—she wept!

"See that. Don't they eat in the city? You're not to go back there until you've been decently fitted out with new feathers. You know what I mean?"

"Yes, grandmother."

"And your mother? And your father? They're all well at home?"

She waited for me to give her news of each one of them before she would set me down again.

"The journey hasn't overtired him?" she would ask my uncle.

"Not at all. We moved like tortoises, and here he is, ready to run as fast as a hare."

Then, only half-convinced, she would take me by the hand, and we would set out toward the village. I entered between my grandmother and my uncle, holding each by the hand. When we reached the first huts, my grandmother would shout:

"Good people! My little husband has arrived!"

The women would come out of their huts and run toward us, crying joyfully:

"But he's a regular little man. That's actually a little husband you have there."

They kept picking me up to embrace me. They examined my face closely, and not only my face but my city clothes which, they said, were quite splendid. They said that my grandmother was very lucky to have a little husband like me.

They rushed up from all sides as if the chief of the canton in person were making his entrance into Tindican. And my grandmother smiled with pleasure.

I was greeted in this way at each hut and I returned the greeting of the women with an exuberance equaling theirs. Then, as it was my turn, I gave news about my parents. It used to take us two hours to cover the one or two hundred metres between my grandmother's hut and the first huts we had passed on the outskirts of the village. And when these excellent women *did* leave us, they went to oversee the cooking of enormous dishes of rice and fowl which they must bring us in time for the evening's feast.

My uncle's concession was enormous. If there were fewer inhabitants and it was less important than ours, it spread out nonetheless over an extensive countryside. There were corrals for the cows and goats, and granaries for rice and millet, for manioc, earth-nuts, and gombo. The granaries were like so many little huts built on stone foundations to keep out the dampness. Except for them, and for the corrals, my uncle's concession was much like ours, but the wooden fence which protected it was stronger. In place of woven reeds, they had used heavy stakes which had been cut in the neighboring forest. The huts, though built like ours, were more primitive.

Since my uncle Lansana was the eldest son, he had inherited the concession when my grandfather died. Actually he had a twin who might have inherited it, but Lansana had been born first. Among my people the twin born first is the elder. On occasion the rights of the elder twin may be abrogated, for when there are twins one of them always has a stronger character than the other, and when this is the case—even if he is not the first-born—he becomes the heir.

As for my uncles, the twin born last might have been the heir, for he lacked neither prestige nor authority. But he had other ideas. He had no taste for farming and was rarely seen at Tindican. He led a roving life, and we knew where he was only by chance or when he made one of his infrequent visits. He had a taste for adventure. I saw him only once. He had returned to Tindican, and though he had been there only a few days, he thought of nothing but leaving it. I remember him as a most attractive man who talked a great deal. Indeed, he never stopped talking, and I never wearied of listening to him. He told me about his adventures, which were strange and bewildering, but which opened undreamed of vistas to me. He showered me with gifts. Was he taking special pains to please this schoolboy—for that was all I was —or was he naturally generous? I do not know. When I saw him leave for new adventures, I wept. What was his name? I don't remember. Perhaps I never knew it. The few days he was at Tindican, I called him Bo, but this was also the name by which I called my uncle Lansana. Twins are always called "Bo," and this surname often makes people forget their proper names.

Lansana had two other brothers, one of whom had recently been married. The younger, the one who came to fetch me from Kouroussa, was engaged but still too young to marry. Thus it happened that two small families, those of each married uncle, also lived in the concession in addition to my grandmother and my youngest uncle.

Usually when I arrived in the afternoon, my uncle Lan

sana was still in the fields, and I went immediately to my grandmother's hut where I was to stay while at Tindican.

The inside of this hut resembled the one I shared at Kouroussa with my mother. There was even a calabash like my mother's for storing milk, covered like ours to keep out the soot, and hung in exactly the same way from the roof by three ropes, so that the farm animals could not get at it. What made this hut remarkable, so far as I was concerned, were the ears of corn hung high in innumerable garlands, so arranged that they grew smaller and smaller as they reached the roof-top. The fire smoked the corn and protected it from termites and mosquitoes. These garlands could have been used as a rustic calendar: as harvest-time approached, their number decreased, and finally they disappeared entirely.

On these visits I only entered the hut to leave my clothes there. My grandmother thought that since I had traveled from Kouroussa to Tindican, it was first necessary for her to wash me. She wanted me clean, though she had no illusions I would remain that way. At least, she wanted me to begin my visit clean. She took me immediately to the bathing place, a small enclosed space near her hut, fenced in with reeds and paved with large stones. Then she went back to her hut, removed the pot from the fire, and poured the hot water into a calabash. When it had cooled to the right temperature, she brought it out, soaped me from head to foot with black soap, and rubbed me vigorously with a hempen sponge. The blood coursed through my veins, my face shone, and my hair was very black (for the dust had been washed out of it) as I left the hut and ran to dry myself in front of the fire.

My playmates would be there waiting for me.

"You have come back."

"I have come back."

"For long?"

"For a while."

Then, depending on whether I was thin or plump—for they too considered looks most important—but I was usually thin—I would hear:

"You're looking well."

"Yes."

Or:

"But you aren't plump!"

"I'm growing. When you're growing you can't be plump."

"That's so. But you aren't plump enough."

And they would fall silent for a while as they considered this growing period which makes city children thinner than country children. Then one of them would shout:

"Look at the birds in the fields!"

This happened every year. There were always great flocks of birds attacking the crops and it was our chief task to drive them away.

"I have my slingshot," I would say.

I had brought it with me, never letting it out of my sight all the way, nor did I while I was at Tindican—not even when I was grazing the cattle or watching the crops from the top of the lookout posts.

These posts played a very important part in my visits: they were platforms mounted on forked stakes, and looked as if they were borne up by the rising tide of the harvest. They were everywhere. My playmates and I would mount the ladder to one of them and aim with our slingshots at the birds and sometimes at the monkeys which were destroying the crops. At least that was what we were supposed to do, and we did so without grumbling, either because it pleased us, or because we felt it was our duty. Occasionally, we became absorbed in other games, and forgot why we were there. If I did not suffer for this forgetfulness, my playmates did; their parents were not slow to discover that the crops were not being watched, and then—depending on how much damage had been done—a sharp scolding or whipping summoned the neglectful watchmen back to vigilance. Duly instructed in this way, we managed to keep an eye on the crops, even if we were forever gossiping about matters hidden from our parents—usually our childish misdeeds. But our cries and songs often sufficed to drive off the birds—all except the millet-eaters who descended upon the fields in dense flocks.

My playmates were extremely kind. They were excellent companions though stronger than I and, indeed, rather tough. In deference to the city boy sharing their country games, they gladly kept their high spirits in control. Furthermore, they were full of admiration for my school clothes.

As soon as I had dried myself in front of the fire, I dressed. Filled with envy, my playmates watched me put on my short-sleeved khaki shirt, shorts of the same color, and sandals. I also had a beret, which I hardly ever wore. The other clothes made enough of an impression. These splendors dazzled country boys whose sole article of clothing was a short pair of drawers. I envied them their freedom of movement. My city clothes, of which I had to be careful, were a great nuisance, for they might become dirty or torn. When we climbed to the lookout posts, I had to keep from getting caught on the rungs of the ladders. Once on top I had to stay away from the freshly cut ears of corn which were stored there, safe from the termites, and which would later be used as seed. And if we lighted a fire to cook the lizards or field-mice we had killed, I dared not go too close lest the blood stain my clothes or the ashes dirty them. I could only look on as our catch was cleaned and the insides salted, preparatory to being placed on the live coals. And I had to take all sorts of precautions when I ate.

How I would have liked to have rid myself of those school clothes fit only for city wear; and I most certainly would have, had I had anything else to wear. I had come to the country to run about, to play, to scale the lookout posts, and to lose myself in the tall grass with the herds of cattle, and of course I could not do any of these things without spoiling my precious clothes.

As night fell, my uncle Lansana returned from the fields. He greeted me in his usual shy fashion. He had very little to say for himself. It is easy for men who work in the fields all day long to fall into the habit of silence as they mull endlessly over one thing and another. The mystery of things, their how and why, conduces to silence. It is enough for such men to observe things and recognize their impenetrability. You can see this state of mind reflected in their eyes. My uncle Lansana's glance was astonishingly sharp when it lighted on something. But this rarely occurred. He remained entirely preoccupied, still in that reverie which he indulged in endlessly in the fields.

When we were all together at mealtimes, I often stared at him. Usually after a time I was able to catch his eye. This pleased me, for my uncle was goodness itself, and, beside that, he loved me. I think he loved me as much as my grandmother did. I would return his shy smile and sometimes—I always ate very slowly—I would forget to eat.

"You aren't eating," my grandmother would say.

"I am too eating."

"Good. You must eat everything here."

But it would have been impossible to eat all the servings of meat and rice which had been cooked to celebrate my happy arrival. Not that my playmates were unwilling to help. They had been invited and came eagerly, bringing with them the appetites of young wolves. But there was too much food. It could never be consumed.

"Look how round my belly is!" I would hear myself saying.

Our bellies *were* round, and, seated close to the fire as we were, and stuffed with food, we would have fallen asleep had we been less full of energy. But we wanted to have a palaver like our elders. We hadn't seen one another for weeks, perhaps months. We had many things, many new stories to tell one another, and this was the time for them.

In this fashion my first day in the country would end, unless someone brought out the tom-tom, for this was a special occasion. At Tindican the tom-tom was not heard *every* night.

FOUR

December, dry and beautiful, the season of the rice harvest, always found me at Tindican, for this was the occasion of a splendid and joyful festival, to which I was always invited, and I would impatiently wait for my young uncle to come for me. The festival had no set date, since it awaited the ripening of the rice, and this, in turn, depended on the good will of the weather. Perhaps it depended still more on the good will of the genii of the soil, whom it was necessary to consult. If their reply was favorable, the genii, on the day before the harvest, were again supplicated to provide a clear sky and protection for the reapers, who would be in danger of snakebite.

On the day of the harvest, the head of each family went at dawn to cut the first swath in his field. As soon as the first fruits had been gathered, the tom-tom signaled that the harvest had begun. This was the custom; I could not have said then why it was kept and why the signal was only given after the cutting of a swath from each field. I knew that it was customary and inquired no further. Yet, like all our customs, this one had its significance, which I could have discovered by asking the old villagers who retained this kind of knowledge deep in their hearts and memories. But I was not old enough nor curious enough to inquire, nor did I become so until I was no longer in Africa.

Today I am inclined to believe that these first swaths destroyed the inviolability of the fields. I do not remember that the reaping went in any particular direction, or if any offerings were made to the genii. Sometimes only the spirit of a tradition survives; sometimes only its form. Its outer garments, as it were, remain. Was that what was involved here? I can not say. Although my visits to Tindican were frequent, I never stayed long enough to acquire a thorough knowledge of all that went on there. All I know is that the tom-tom sounded only after the first fruits had been gathered, and that we eagerly awaited the signal because we wanted to begin the work and escape into the refreshing shade of the great trees and the biting air of the dawn.

Once the signal had been given, the reapers set out. With them, I marched along to the rhythm of the tom-tom. The young men threw their sickles into the air and caught them as they fell. They shouted simply for the pleasure of shouting, and danced as they followed the tom-tom players. I suppose it would have been wise to heed my grandmother's advice. She had warned me not to be too friendly with these players. But it would have been impossible for me to have torn myself away from their spirited music, from their sickles flashing in the rising sun, from the sweetness of the air and the crescendo of the tom-toms.

The season itself would not permit it. In December, everything is in flower. Everything is young. Spring and summer seem inseparable and, everywhere, the country, which, until now has been drenched with rain and dulled by heavy clouds, lies radiant. The sky has never been clearer nor brighter. Birds sing ecstatically. Joy is everywhere, erupts everywhere, and every heart is moved by it. This season, this beautiful season, stirred me deeply. And so did the tom-tom and the festal air that our march acquired. It was a beautiful season, and everything in it—what wasn't there in it? what didn't it pour forth in profusion?—delighted me.

When they had reached the first field, the men lined up at the edge, naked to the loins, their sickles ready. My uncle Lansana or some other farmer—for the harvest threw people together and everyone helped everyone else—would signal that the work was to begin. Immediately, the black torsos would bend over the great golden field, and the sickles begin to cut. Now it was not only the morning breeze which made the field tremble, but also the men working.

The movement of the sickles as they rose and fell was astonishingly rapid and regular. They had to cut off the stalk between the last joint and the last leaf at the same time that they stripped the leaf. They almost never missed. This was largely due to the way the reaper held the stalks so as to cut them. Nonetheless, the speed of the sickle was astonishing. Each man made it a point of honor to reap as regularly and as rapidly as possible. As he moved across the field he had a bundle of stalks in his hand. His fellows judged him by the number and size of these bundles.

My young uncle was wonderful at rice-cutting, the very best. I followed him proudly, step by step, he handing me the bundles of stalks as he cut them. I tore off the leaves, trimmed the stalks, and piled them. Since rice is always harvested when it is very ripe, and, if handled roughly the grains drop off, I had to be very careful. Tying the bundles into sheaves was man's work, but, when they had been tied, I was allowed to put them on the pile in the middle of the field.

As the morning drew on, it became hotter. The air seemed to shimmer in a thick haze which was composed of a fine veil of dust from the trampled sod and the stubble. My uncle would wipe the sweat from his chest and forehead and ask for his water-jug. I would run to fetch it from under the leaves where it lay, all fresh and cool, and would bring it to him.

"Be sure to leave some for me," I would remind him.

"Don't worry; I won't drink all of it."

He would take great swallows without touching the jug to his lips. "There now. That's better," he would say, handing me the jug. "This dust is sticking in my throat."

I would touch my lips to the jug, and immediately the freshness of the water would permeate my body. But refreshment was only momentary, for it passed quickly and left me covered with sweat.

"Take your shirt off," my uncle would say. "You're soaking wet. You shouldn't keep wet things on your chest."

And he set to work again, and once again I followed him, proud to see that we were ahead of the others.

"Aren't you getting tired?" I would ask him.

"Why should I be tired?"

"Your sickle moves so quickly."

"It does, doesn't it?"

"We're ahead of the rest."

"Yes?"

"You know we are. Why do you question it?"

"One shouldn't boast."

"No."

And I would ask myself if some day I would be able to do as well.

"May I reap for a while?"

"What would your grandmother say? This sickle is no toy. You have no idea how sharp it is."

"I do."

"It isn't your job to cut rice. I don't think it ever will be. Later . . ."

I didn't like the fact that he thought the field work not for me. "Later . . . !" Why "later . . . ?" It seemed to me that I too could become a reaper like the rest, a farmer like them. Was it that . . . ?

"You're day-dreaming?" my uncle would interrupt.

And I would take the bundle of stalks he handed me, strip off the leaves, and trim the stalks. It was true that I had been day-dreaming: my life did not lie here . . . and I had no life in my father's forge. But where was my life? And I trembled at the thought of the unknown life ahead of me. Wouldn't it be simpler to take up my father's work? "School . . . school . . ." I thought. After all, was I so fond of school? Perhaps I did prefer it. My uncles. . . . Yes, certainly I had uncles who had followed in their father's footsteps without complaint. Others had taken a different course: my father's brothers had gone to Conakry; my Uncle Lansana's brother was. . . . Where was he now?

"Do you spend all your time day-dreaming?" my uncle would ask.

"Yes. . . . No. . . . I. . . ."

"If you keep this up, we won't be ahead any longer."

"I was thinking about Uncle Bo. Where is he now?"

"God knows. When he was here last he was. . . . But I don't even know where he was! He's like a bird, never in the same place, can't stay on one tree. He needs the whole sky."

"Will I too be like a bird some day?"

"What's that?"

"But you just said Bo was like a bird."

"Do you want to be like him?"

"I don't know."

"Well, there's still time for you to make up your mind. Meanwhile, take this bundle."

And he started reaping again. He was dripping wet, but he returned to his work energetically, as if he were just beginning. And the heat bore down on us. The very air bore down. Fatigue suffused our bodies. Tumblers full of water couldn't have kept it away. We battled it with song.

"Sing with us," my uncle would command.

The tom-tom, which had followed as we advanced into the field, kept time with our voices. We sang as a chorus, now very high-pitched with great bursts of song, and then very low, so low we could scarcely be heard. Our fatigue vanished, and the heat became less oppressive.

On such occasions, if I happened to stop work for a moment and look at that long, long line of reapers, I was always impressed and carried away by the infinite love and kindliness of their eyes, as they glanced here and there. Yet, though their glances were also distant and preoccupied, though they seemed miles from their task, they never slighted it. Hands and sickles moved without interruption.

And, what actually *were* they looking at? At one another? A likely idea! Perhaps at the distant trees or the still more distant sky. And again, perhaps not. Perhaps they were looking at nothing. Perhaps there was nothing to look at, and this only made them seem distant and preoccupied. The long line of reapers hurled itself at the field and hewed it down. Wasn't that enough? Wasn't it enough that the rice bowed before these black bodies? They sang and they reaped. Singing in chorus, they reaped, voices and gestures in harmony. They were together!—united by the same task, the same song. It was as if the same soul bound them.

Was it pleasure, and not the combat against fatigue and heat, that urged them on, singing? Obviously. The same pleasure filled their eyes with that lovingness which had struck me, delightfully and a little regretfully, for though I was near them, part of them, I was not entirely one of them:

I was a schoolboy on a visit; how gladly I would have forgotten that fact.

Indeed, I did forget it, for I was still very young. What crossed my mind—so many things were always crossing it—was more fleeting and less enduring than the clouds which cross the sky. I was then at the age—I have always been that age—when one lives entirely in the present, when being first in a long line of reapers was more important than my future.

"Hurry up!" I would urge my uncle.

"Well! You're awake?"

"Yes. Let's not waste time."

"Was *I* wasting it?"

"No, but you might. We aren't so much ahead now."

"Don't you think so?"

And he would look at the crop.

"Is this what you call not being so far ahead of the others? I haven't wasted any time, but perhaps I should now. Don't forget that I must not get too far ahead of the others; it would offend them."

I do not know how the idea of something rustic—I use the word in its accepted meaning: "lack of finesse, of delicacy"—became associated with country people. Civil formalities are more respected on the farm than in the city. Farm ceremony and manners are not understood by the city, which has no time for these things. To be sure, farm life is simpler than city life. But dealings between one man and another—perhaps because in the country everyone knows everyone else—are more strictly regulated. I used to notice a dignity everywhere which I have rarely found in cities. One did not act without duly considering such action, even though it were an entirely personal affair. The rights of others were highly respected. And if intelligence seemed slower it was because reflection preceded speech and because speech itself was a most serious matter.

At noon, the women, bearing smoking platters of *couscous*, left the village and walked, single file, to the field. As soon as we saw them we greeted them noisily. Noon! It was noon! And work stopped all over the field.

"Let's go!" my uncle would urge me.

And I would bound off after him.

"Not so fast! I can't keep up with you."

"Don't you have a hole in your stomach? I could stable an ox in mine."

And our appetites were in fact marvelously sharp. The heat could be very strong and the field, with its dust and its shimmering haze, might have been a furnace, but that did not interfere with our appetites. We sat around the platters, and the hot *couscous*, even hotter because of the spices in it, disappeared, washed down by tumblers of fresh water which had been drawn from the great jars covered with banana leaves.

For two hours no one did anything. The men spent the time sleeping under the trees or sharpening their sickles. Since we were not at all tired, my playmates and I gamboled about and went off to set snares. Although we made a great deal of noise as usual, we were careful, because the men were reaping, not to whistle or pick up dead wood: for fear of bringing misfortune to the farm.

The afternoon's work was much shorter and passed rapidly. It was five o'clock before we knew it. Having stripped the

great field of its treasure, we marched back to the village
—the tall silk-cotton trees and the smoke from the huts signaled that it was time to do so. We marched, preceded by
the indefatigable tom-tom player, and we sang the song of
the rice.

Above us the swallows were already flying lower, and,
although the air was as clear as ever, the end of the day was
near. We were happy as we entered the village, weary and
happy. The geniis had taken good care of us: not one of us
had been bitten by snakes dislodged when we trampled the
field. The scent of flowers, awakened by the approach of
evening, seemed to clothe us in fresh garlands. If our song
had been less noisy we would have heard the familiar sounds
of the day's end: cries and laughter mingled with the lowing
of cattle returning to the corral. But we were singing. We
were singing. Ah! How happy we were in those days!

FIVE

At Kouroussa I lived in my mother's hut. But, since the huts were so small, my brothers and sisters, all of whom were younger than I, slept in my father's mother's hut. My mother kept my brothers and sisters in her hut while nursing them. But as soon as they were weaned—among my people children are weaned very late—she turned them over to my grandmother. I was the only one of her children who lived with her. But I did not have the second bed to myself: I shared it with my father's youngest apprentices.

My father always had lots of apprentices in his workshop; they came from far and near, often from very remote districts, mainly, I think, because he treated them well, but above all because his skill as a craftsman was widely acknowledged, and also, I imagine, because there was always plenty of work at his forge. But these apprentices had to have somewhere to sleep.

Those who had reached manhood had their own hut. The youngest, those who, like me, were still uncircumcised, slept in my mother's hut. My father certainly thought they could have no better lodging. My mother was very kind, very correct. She also had great authority, and kept an eye on everything we did; so that her kindness was not altogether untempered by severity. But how could it have been otherwise, when there were at that time, apart from the apprentices, a dozen children running about the concession, children who were not good all the time, but always so full of life that they must often have sorely tried their mother's patience—and my mother was not a very patient woman.

I see now that she was more patient with the apprentices than she was with her own children. She put herself out for them more than she did for us. These apprentices were far from home, and both my mother and father were very affectionate with them, coddling them like babies, and indulging them more than they did their own children. My mother's chief concern I certainly was, but she did not show it. The apprentices were encouraged to believe themselves on an equal footing with the master's children. I thought of them as elder brothers.

I remember one of them particularly: Sidafa. He was a little older than myself, very lively, thin but vigorous, hot-blooded, always full of projects and ideas of every kind. As my days were spent at school, and his in the workshop, the only time we had for chattering was when we went to bed. The air in the hut was warm, and the oil lamps at the side of the bed cast a dim light. I would repeat to Sidafa what I had been learning at school: and he for his part would recount in detail all that had gone on in the workshop. My mother, whose bed was separated from ours only by the width of the hearth, had of necessity to listen to our chatter. At least she listened for a while but soon wearied of it.

"Have you gone to bed to chatter or to sleep?" she would say. "Go to sleep!"

"Just a minute. I haven't finished my story," I would plead.

Or I would get up and take a drink of water to the canary who had gone dry as he perched over his bed of gravel. But the reprieve I asked for was not always granted, and, when it was, we took such advantage of it that my mother would interrupt us sharply:

"Now that's enough!" she would say. "I don't want to hear another word! You'll neither of you be able to get up in the morning."

Which was true: if we were never in any great hurry to go to sleep, neither were we ever in any great hurry to get up. We would stop chattering. The beds were too near to my mother's sharp ears for us to be able to talk in whispers. And, then, as soon as we were quiet, we very quickly felt our eyes grow weary; the cozy crackling of the fire and the warmth of the bedclothes did the rest: we gradually drifted into sleep.

In the morning when, after some persuasion, we rose, we

found the breakfast ready. My mother awoke at dawn to prepare it. We all sat around the great steaming dishes: my parents, sisters, brothers, and the apprentices, those who shared my bed as well as those who had their own hut. There was one dish for the men, and another for my mother and my sisters.

It would not be exactly right for me to say that my mother presided over the meal: my father presided over it. Nevertheless, it was the presence of my mother that made itself felt first of all. Was that because she had prepared the food, because meals are things which are mainly a woman's business? Maybe. But there was something more: my mother, by the mere fact of her presence, and even though she was not seated directly in front of the men's dish, saw to it that everything was done according to her own rules; and those rules were strict.

Thus it was forbidden to cast my gaze upon guests older than myself, and I was also forbidden to talk: my whole attention had to be fixed on the food before me. In fact, it would have been most impolite to chatter at that moment. Even my younger brothers knew that this was no time to jabber: this was the hour to pay honor to the food. Older people observed more or less the same silence. This was not the only rule: those concerning cleanliness were no less important. Finally, if there was meat on the dish, I was not allowed to take it from the centre of the dish, but only from the part directly in front of me, and my father would put more within my reach if he saw I needed it. Any other behavior would have been frowned upon and quickly reprimanded. In any case, my portion was always so plentiful that

I should never have been tempted to take more than I was given.

When the meal was over, I would say: "Thank you, Father."

The apprentices would say: "Thank you, master."

Then I would bow to my mother and say: "The meal was good, Mother."

My brothers, my sisters, the apprentices did likewise. My parents replied, "Thank you," to each one of them. Such was the rule. My father would certainly have been offended to see it broken, but it was my mother, with her quicker temper, who rebuked any transgression. My father's mind was with his work, and he left these prerogatives to her.

I realize that my mother's authoritarian attitudes may appear surprising; generally the role of the African woman is thought to be a ridiculously humble one, and indeed there are parts of the continent where it is insignificant; but Africa is vast, with a diversity equal to its vastness. The woman's role in our country is one of fundamental independence, of great inner pride. We despise only those who allow themselves to be despised; and our women very seldom give cause for that. My father would never have dreamed of despising anyone, least of all my mother. He had the greatest respect for her too, and so did our friends and neighbors. That was due, I am sure, to my mother's character, which was impressive; it was due also to the strange powers she possessed.

I hesitate to say what these powers were, and I do not wish to describe them all. I know that what I say will be greeted with skeptical smiles. And today, now that I come to remember them, even I hardly know how I should regard them. They seem to be unbelievable; they *are* unbelievable. Nevertheless I can only tell you what I saw with my own eyes. How can I disown the testimony of my own eyes? Those unbelievable things. I saw them. I see them again as I saw them then. Are there not things around us, everywhere, which are inexplicable? In our country there were mysteries without number, and my mother was familiar with them all.

One day—it was toward evening—I saw some men request her to use her powers to get a horse on his feet after he had resisted all attempts to make him rise. He was out at pasture, but he was lying down, and his owner wanted to bring him back to the stable before nightfall. The horse obstinately refused to move, although there was no apparent reason why he should disobey. But his inclination was otherwise, though it might have been a magic spell that immobilized him. I heard the men telling my mother about it, and asking her help.

"Well, then, let's go and have a look at this horse," said my mother.

She called the eldest of my sisters and told her to look after the cooking of the evening meal, and then went off with the men. I followed her. When we arrived at the pasture, we saw the horse: he was lying in the grass, gazing at us unconcernedly. His owner tried again to make him get up and spoke to him in honeyed tones, but the horse remained deaf to all entreaty. His master raised a hand to strike him.

"Do not strike him," said my mother. "It won't do any good."

She went up to the horse and, lifting her own hand, declaimed in a solemn tone: "If it is true that from the day of my birth I had knowledge of no man until the day of my marriage: and if it is true that from the day of my marriage I have had knowledge of no man other than my lawful husband—if these things be true, then I command you, horse, rise up!"

And we all saw the horse get up at once and follow his master quietly away. I have told in very simple words, and very exact words, what I saw then, with my own eyes, and to my mind it is unbelievable; but the event was just as I have described it: the horse got up without any further delay and followed his master: if he had refused to follow him, my mother's intervention would once more have had its effect.

Where did these powers come from? Well, my mother was the next child born after my twin uncles in Tindican. Now, they say that twin brothers are wiser than other children, and are practically magicians. As for the child that follows them, and who receives the name *sayon*, that is, the younger brother of twins, he too is endowed with the gift of magic, and he is even considered to be more powerful and more mysterious than the twins in whose lives he plays a very important role. So if twins fall out, it is to the *sayon's* authority that one appeals to settle the matter; indeed, he is accredited with a wisdom greater than that of the twins, and is given a superior position. It goes without saying that his intervention is conducted, must be conducted, in the most tactful way.

It is the custom with us for twins to agree about everything, and they are to have by right a more precise equality of treatment than is accorded to other children: if something is given to one the other must be given the same thing also. It is an obligation which must never be disregarded; if it is, the twins are equally hurt, settle the matter between themselves, and in certain cases cast a spell upon the person who has injured them. If any kind of dispute should arise between them—if one, for example, has a plan which the other thinks is foolish—they make an appeal to their younger brother and are happy to accept his decision.

I don't know if my mother had often had to intervene between my twin uncles, but even if she did so infrequently it was still enough to lead her, very early in life, to weigh the pros and cons of things and to make her own judgments. If it was said of the *sayon* that he was wiser than his twin brothers, the reason was clear: the *sayon* assumed heavier responsibilities than the twins.

I have given one example of my mother's supernatural powers; I could give many others, equally strange, equally mysterious. How many times I have seen her, at daybreak, walk a few steps into the yard and turn her head in one direction or another to shout at the top of her voice:

"If this business goes any further, I shall not hesitate to expose you. That's my final word!"

In the early morning her voice traveled far: it was intended to reach the ears of the witch-doctor, for whom the warning had been uttered. He understood that if he did not stop his nocturnal activities, my mother would denounce him in public; and this threat always worked: from then on, the witch-doctor kept quiet. My mother used to receive warning of these activities while she was asleep. We never wakened her, for fear of interrupting the course of the revelations that flowed through her dreams. This power was well known by our neighbors and by the whole communtity: no one ever doubted it.

Though my mother could see what evil was being hatched and could denounce the author of it, her power went no further. Even if she had wished, her power to cast spells did not allow her to do any evil on her own account. She was never suspect. If people made themselves pleasant to her, it was not at all out of fear. They were pleasant because they thought she deserved it, and because they respected her power to cast spells from which nothing was to be feared. On the contrary, much was to be hoped from them.

As well as this gift, or rather part-gift, of magic, my mother had other powers that she had inherited in the same way. At Tindican her father had been a skillful blacksmith, and my mother possessed the usual powers of that caste from which the majority of circumcisers and many soothsayers are drawn. My mother's brothers had chosen to be farmers, but if they had not followed their father's trade that was their own affair. Perhaps my Uncle Lansana, the silent one who was a great dreamer, in fixing his choice upon a farm-worker's life, upon the immense peace of the fields, had led his brothers away from the paternal forge. Was he, also, a soothsayer? I am inclined to think he was. He had the customary powers of a twin, and the powers of his caste; only I do not think that he exhibited them very often. I have already spoken of how reserved his manner was, of how much he liked to be alone with his thoughts, of how absent-minded he seemed. No. He was not the man to make a display of these powers. It was in my mother that the spirit of her caste was most visibly—I was going to say ostensibly—manifested. I don't pretend that she was more faithful to it than my uncles were, but she alone demonstrated her fidelity. Finally, she had inherited, as a matter of course, my grandfather's totem which is the crocodile. This totem allowed all Damans to draw water from the Niger without running any danger of harm.

Normally, everyone draws water from the river. The Niger flows slowly and abundantly; it can be forded; and the crocodiles, which keep to the deep water upstream or downstream from where the water is drawn, are not to be feared. You can bathe quite freely on the banks of pale sand and do your washing there.

But when the water rises, the volume of the river is increased three-fold. The water is deep, and the crocodiles are dangerous. One can see their triangular heads breaking the surface. Everyone, therefore, keeps away from the river and instead draws water from the little streams.

My mother used to continue to draw water from the river. I watched her draw it from the place where the crocodiles were. Naturally I watched her from a distance, for my totem is not my mother's. And I had every reason to fear those voracious beasts; but my mother could draw water without fear, and no one warned her of the danger, because everyone knew that the danger did not exist for her. Whoever else had ventured to do what my mother used to do would inevitably have been knocked down by a blow from a powerful tail, seized in the terrible jaws and dragged into deep water. But the crocodiles could do no harm to my mother; and this privilege is quite understandable: the totem is identified with its possessor: this identification is absolute, and of such a nature that its possessor has the power to take on the form of the totem itself; it follows quite obviously that the totem can not devour itself. My uncles at Tindican enjoyed the same prerogative.

I do not wish to say more, and I have told you only what I saw with my own eyes. These miracles—they were miracles indeed—I think about now as if they were the fabulous events of a far-off past. That past is, however, still quite near: it was only yesterday. But the world rolls on, the world changes, my own world perhaps more rapidly than anyone else's; so that it appears as if we are ceasing to be what we were, and that truly we are no longer what we were, and that we were not exactly ourselves even at the time when these miracles took place before our eyes. Yes, the world rolls on, the world changes; it rolls on and changes, and the proof of it is that my own totem—I too have my totem—is still unknown to me.

SIX

I was very young when I began school, first attending the Koran school, and, shortly afterwards, transferring to the French. Neither my mother nor I had the slightest suspicion how long I would be a student in the latter. Had she known, I am sure she would have kept me at home. Perhaps my father knew already.

Immediately after breakfast my sister and I would start out, carrying our books and notebooks in a raffia satchel. On the way we would be joined by our friends, and the closer we got to school the more of us there would be. My sister walked with the girls, I stayed with the boys. Like all young boys we loved to tease the girls, but they gave as good as they got, and when we pulled their hair they fought back, scratching and biting us, although this did not dampen our enthusiasm noticeably. There was, however, a truce between my sister and myself; her friend, Fanta, also let me alone, but I did not return the compliment.

One day when we were alone in the school yard, she asked me, "Why do you pull my hair?"

"Because you're a girl."

"I don't pull yours."

I stopped to think for a moment. Only then did I realize that she was the only one, with the exception of my sister, who didn't.

"Well, why don't you?" I asked.

"Because!"

"Because! What kind of an answer's that?"

"I wouldn't hurt you, no matter what."

"Well, I'm going to pull *your* hair."

But then it seemed foolish to do it when none of my classmates was around. She burst into laughter when I did not carry out my threat.

"You just wait until school's out," I threatened.

But again I did not make good my threat. Something restrained me, and from then on I rarely bothered her. My sister was not long in noticing this.

"I don't see you pulling Fanta's hair," she said.

"Why should I? She leaves me alone."

"Yes, I've noticed."

"Then, why should I?"

"Oh, I don't know. I thought there might be some other reason."

What was she getting at? I shrugged my shoulders. Girls were crazy; all girls were.

"Oh, Fanta makes me sick," I said. "And you make me sick too."

She only laughed at me.

"Now, you watch out," I said. "If you don't stop laughing—"

She avoided my grasp and shouted from a distance: "Fanta! Fanta!"

"Oh, shut up."

She paid no attention to me, and I rushed at her.

"Fanta! Fanta!"

Unfortunately I couldn't find a stone to throw at her, but I made a resolution to take care of that matter later.

Once at school, we went straight to our seats, boys and girls side by side, their quarrels over. So motionless and attentive did we sit, that it would have been wonderful to see what would have happened had we stirred. Our teacher moved like quicksilver, here, there, everywhere. His flow of talk would have bewildered less attentive pupils; but we were extraordinarily attentive. Young though we were, we regarded our school work as a deadly serious matter. Nothing that we learned was old or expected; all came as though from another planet, and we never tired of listening. But even if we had wearied, this omnipresent teacher would never have given us an opportunity to interrupt. Interruption was out of the question; the idea did not even occur to us. We wanted to be noticed as little as possible, for we lived in continual dread of being sent to the blackboard.

This was our nightmare. The blackboard's blank surface was an exact replica of our minds. We knew little, and the little that we knew came out haltingly. The slightest thing could inhibit us. When we were called to the blackboard we had to take the chalk and really work, if we were to avoid a beating. The smallest detail was of the utmost importance, and the blackboard magnified everything. If we made one downward stroke not precisely of the same height as the others, we were required to do extra lessons on Sunday, or were sent during recess to the first grade for a caning—a caning, I should add, one did not easily forget. Irregular downward strokes made our teacher furious. He examined our exercises under a magnifying glass, and dealt out his blows accordingly. He was indeed quicksilver, and he wielded his rod with joyous *élan*.

This was how things were in the primary grades. There were fewer beatings in the upper classes; other kinds of punishment, no more pleasant, took their place. I underwent a vast variety of punishments in that school, and only one thing did not vary—my anguish. One's love of knowledge had to be very strong to survive these ordeals.

For second-year students, the customary punishment was sweeping the school yard. It was then that we comprehended how truly spacious that yard was, what an enormous number of guava trees it possessed. It seemed to us certain that the trees had been planted there for the specific purpose of littering the ground, for certainly we never received any of the fruit. In the third and fourth years our punishment was to work in the kitchen garden; and it would have been difficult to find cheaper labor. During our last two years, the school authorities had such confidence in us—a confidence, I might add, we would have gladly foregone—that we were entrusted with the herd of cattle which belonged to the school.

This last task was no sinecure. The herd we tended was famous for miles around. Did a farmer have a vicious cow, it inevitably ended up in our herd. There was a good reason for this; the farmer, desperate to be rid of the beast, would accept almost any price, and the school authorities were only too anxious to take advantage of such a windfall. So the real reason was stinginess, and the result was that our school owned the most complete collection of sly, ornery creatures in existence. When we cried out, "Right!" it was just natural for them to veer left.

The way they galloped about in the bush, it seemed as if a swarm of flies were constantly irritating them. We galloped after them, incredible distances. They were always much more intent on wandering off, or battling among themselves, than foraging for food. However, their picturesque behavior was no pleasure to us. We knew that, on our return, the school authorities would carefully survey their bellies to see how well they had eaten. And woe to us should the stomachs of those raw-boned creatures not be full.

But heaven help us indeed, should a single head be missing from this, the devil's own herd. We would return home at nightfall, exhausted, since we had to whip them into a lather in order to get them to move at all in the right direction. This, of course, did not improve the dispositions of these fantastic animals. To make up for their not having eaten very much, we would gorge them with water. Footsore, we would appear with the entire herd. We would not have dared come back without every one of them. The consequences would have been too dreadful.

That's how it was with our teachers—at any rate, when things were at their worst—and it is understandable enough that we could scarcely wait to finish school and receive that famous certificate of studies which proclaimed us "learned." And yet it seems that as yet I have scarcely said anything about the dark side of our school life, since the worst was what the older pupils made us younger ones suffer. These older students—I can not call them "comrades" since they were older and stronger than we, and less strictly supervised —persecuted us in every conceivable way. They were a haughty lot, and with reason, since no doubt they were repaying the treatment they had themselves received: Excessively harsh treatment is not precisely the best method of inculcating kindness.

I remember—my hands and fingertips can not forget—what lay in store for us when we returned to school after vacation. The guava trees in the yard would be in leaf again and last year's leaves would be strewn about the ground in scattered heaps. In places there would be great piles of them.

"Sweep these up," the director would say. "This yard must be cleaned immediately."

Immediately! And there was enough work there, damnable work, for more than a week. There was more work than there should have been, since the only tools we had were our hands —our hands, and our fingers, and our fingernails.

"Now, be quick about it," the director would say to the older students, "or you'll be hearing from me."

At an order from the older boys, we would line up like peasants about to reap a field, but we did not work like peasants; we worked like galley slaves. This in a school yard! There were open spaces between the guava trees, but there was also a place where the guava trees grew so close together that their branches intertwined. Here the sun did not penetrate, and the acrid odor of decay lingered when the weather was fine.

Even when the work was not proceeding as quickly as the director had ordered, the older boys refused to help. They considered it easier to pull branches from the trees with which to beat us. Guava wood is extremely flexible, and when skillfully handled the whips whistled as they moved through the air; our backs felt as though they were on fire. Our flesh smarted, and tears fell from our eyes.

There was only one way to avoid these blows, and that was to bribe our tyrants with the lunches we had brought from home; the savory cakes of Indian corn, the wheat, the *couscous* made of meat or fish. If we had any money, that also changed hands. Anyone who refused to give up his lunch, mindful of his empty stomach, found himself the recipient of a dreadful beating. It was administered so violently, in such a diabolical rhythm, that even a deaf man would have understood that these blows were given not to speed up the work but to extort food and money.

Occasionally one of us, worn out by the deliberate cruelty, would dare to complain to the director. The director would become very angry, but the punishment he inflicted on the culprits was nothing compared to what they had administered. At any rate, our complaints did nothing to remedy the situation. Possibly it would have been wiser to have informed our parents of what we were undergoing, but somehow or other this never occurred to us. Perhaps we remained silent because of pride, or because of loyalty to the school. I know now that whatever the reason, it was stupid of us to keep silent. Such beatings were utterly alien to my people's passion for independence and equality.

One day, one of my playmates, Kouyaté Karmoko, having been the recipient of a particularly brutal beating, declared that he had had enough of this sort of thing. Kouyaté was extremely small and thin—so small that we joked that he must have the stomach of a bird, that is, a gizzard. One thing is certain, whether Kouyaté was the owner of a gizzard or some other form of stomach, he put very little into it. He cared only for fruit, and at lunch was satisfied if he were able to trade his *couscous* for guavas and oranges. This minimum even he required, and it was obvious that, if he were forced to give up his fruit, he would inevitably have to turn in his gizzard for something smaller, perhaps the stomach of an insect. This did not bother the older boys; their insistent demands forced Kouyaté into a rigorous period of fasting. That day, hunger, in combination with the welts on his buttocks, made him rebel.

"I've taken all I intend to," he sniffled through his tears. "I'm going to tell my father."

"It won't do you any good to make a fuss," I said.

"You really don't think it will?"

"Don't forget that the older boys—"

But he would not let me finish.

"I don't care—I'm going to tell him," he shouted at the top of his voice.

"For heaven's sakes, keep your voice down."

He was my best friend, and I was afraid that this outburst would only earn him another beating.

"You know my father—you know he'll do something."

I knew Kouyaté's father well, he was one of the most respected praise-singers in the district. Although he no longer practiced his profession, he had a special standing in the community—a sort of scholar and praise-singer emeritus. There was no house that was not open to him.

"Kouyaté, your father's an old man."

"A very strong man," he replied proudly, drawing his thin little body up to its full height.

"You're being stupid," I warned him.

He left off whining, and I finished the conversation by telling him to do as he pleased.

The next day, no sooner had Kouyaté arrived at the school yard than he went over to Himourana, the boy who had thrashed him so brutally the day before.

"My father is most anxious to meet the upper form boy who has been kindest to me. I thought of you at once. Can you come to dinner this evening?"

"I'll be happy to," Himourana said.

Himourana's brutality was only matched by his stupidity. He was probably a glutton as well.

And that evening, sure enough, the dunce showed up at Kouyaté's concession. One of the most sturdily built in Kouroussa, it had only one gate, and the wall around it, instead of being made of reeds, was constructed of masonry with pieces of broken glass strewn along the top. One entered or left it only by permission of the master of the house. That evening Kouyaté's father came to open the gate in person, and, when Himourana had entered it, it was carefully bolted behind him.

"Do sit down," said Kouyaté's father. "Our whole family is expecting you."

Himourana glanced quickly at the cooking utensils, which seemed to promise a most satisfactory meal, and sat down in the yard. He prepared himself for the compliments that were about to be addressed to him. And then Kouyaté arose.

"Father," he said, pointing at the guest. "That's the one who always takes my food and money."

"Now, now, Kouyaté, that's not a nice thing to say," his father replied. "Are you sure you're telling the truth?" And he turned to Himourana. "Young man, you hear what my son has said? What do you have to say in your defense? Do speak quickly. I don't have too much time to give you, but I don't want to be ungenerous."

It was as if a thunderbolt had dropped at Himourana's feet. He couldn't understand a word of what was being said. He thought only of fleeing, which would have been a reasonable enough idea if there had not been that wall. One had to be as big a boob as Himourana to attempt to put the idea into execution. He was caught before he had taken ten steps.

"Now, get this into your head," Kouyaté's father said. "I am not sending my son to school for you to make a slave out of him."

And then Himourana found himself raised aloft by his

arms and legs and held extended, while Kouyaté's father gave him a sound thrashing. Shamefaced, his rear end aflame, he was then permitted to go.

The next day at school the story of Himourana's punishment spread like wildfire. It created a scandal. Never before had such a thing happened, and we could scarcely believe that it had happened. All of us younger boys felt that Kouyaté's father had avenged us. The upshot was that the older boys held a meeting and decided that Kouyaté and his sister, Mariama, were to be ostracized. The edict was extended to us younger students—we also were not to talk to our playmate. However, we noted that they were very careful not to touch either Kouyaté or his sister, and even the stupidest of us was aware that they were afraid. An era had ended, we sensed, and we prepared to breathe the air of liberty.

At noon I went up to Kouyaté, having decided to defy our oppressors.

"Be careful," he said. "You know what's likely to happen."

"Oh, to hell with them."

I gave him the oranges I had brought for lunch.

"Do go away. I'm afraid they'll beat you."

I had no time to answer. Several of them were coming toward us, and I hesitated, unable to decide whether to run or not. I made my decision, and suddenly I felt their blows upon me. Then I ran, and didn't stop until I had come to the other end of the school yard. I cried as much from anger as from pain. When I had left off crying, I found Fanta sitting next to me.

"What are you doing here?"

"I've brought you a wheat-cake."

I took it and ate it almost without noticing what I was eating, although Fanta's mother was famous for making the best wheat-cakes in the district. When I had finished I went and drank some water and washed my face. Then I returned and sat down again.

"I don't like you to sit beside me when I'm crying," I said.

"Were you crying? I didn't notice."

I looked at her. She was lying. Obviously to spare my pride. I smiled at her.

"Do you want another wheat-cake?" she asked.

"No, I'm too angry. Doesn't it make you angry, too?"

"Yes," and her eyes filled with tears.

"I hate them!" I cried. "You can't imagine how I hate them. Do you know what I'm going to do? I'm going to quit school. I'm going to grow up fast, and then I'm going to come back. And for every beating I've received, I'm going to pay them back with a thousand."

She stopped crying and looked at me admiringly.

That evening I sought out my father under the veranda.

"Father, I don't want to go to school any more."

"What?"

"No," I said.

But by this time the scandal had gone the rounds of the concessions in Kouroussa.

"What's going on in that school?" my father asked.

"I'm afraid of the older boys."

"I thought you weren't afraid of anyone."

"I'm afraid of them."

"What do they do to you?"

"They take away our money and eat our lunches."

"Do they? And they whip you?"

"Yes."

"Yes, I'll have a word with those bullies tomorrow. So that's what's up?"

The next day my father and his apprentices accompanied me to school, and they stood with me at the school door. Each time one of the older boys passed, my father asked, "Is that one of them?"

"No," I answered, although there were many among them who had beaten and robbed me. But I was waiting for one boy in particular, the one who had treated me most savagely. When I saw him I cried out, "There's the worst of all."

Without further ado, the apprentices threw themselves on him and stripped him bare. They handled him so roughly that my father had to come to his rescue.

"The director and I are going to have a chat about you," he said. "What I want to find out is whether you bigger fellows are here for any other reason than to beat up the smaller boys and steal their money."

That day the business of not speaking to Kouyaté or his sister ended. They played with us, and none of the older boys attempted to interfere. They did not even seem to notice us. Was a new era beginning? It seemed so. The older boys kept to themselves; it seemed almost, since we were the more numerous, that they were the ones who were being ostracized. That they were none too pleased with the way things were going was evident. And certainly they were in none too happy a situation. Up to now their parents had been unaware of their nasty practices. If the parents were informed—and there was a very good chance that everything would become public

—the culprits could expect only scoldings and punishments.

When school was recessed that afternoon, my father arrived. As he had said he would, he went immediately to the director who was in the yard with the other teachers. Without bothering to say: "Good-day," my father asked, "do you have any idea what's going on in this school?"

"Why, of course I do," the director answered. "Everything's proceeding as it should."

"Then the older boys are supposed to whip the younger ones and steal their money? Are you blind, or is that really your intention?"

"Why don't you stay out of what doesn't concern you?"

"Doesn't concern me? Is it no concern of mine that my son is treated like a slave?"

"It most certainly is not."

"That you shouldn't have said!"

And my father marched closer to the director.

"Now I suppose I'm to be beaten the way your apprentices beat one of my students this morning," said the director.

He put up his fists. He was a strong man but quite fat, and my father, who was slender and quick, would have had no trouble with him at all. In fact, he did knock him down, but the assistants pulled them apart before the thing really got under way.

The director stood feeling his jaw and saying nothing; and my father, having dusted himself off, took me by the hand and led me from the yard. I walked proudly beside him to our concession. But later I felt much less proud, when, walking by myself in the city, I heard people say as I passed,

"Look! There's the boy whose father beat up the director in the school yard."

This was not at all comparable to the incident in which Kouyaté's father had been involved. This was a scandal, occurring as it had in the presence of the teachers and students, and with the director as the principal victim. No, it was not at all like the other, and it seemed to me lucky if it should end with no more than my being expelled from school. I hurried back to my father.

"Why did you have to fight with him? I'll never be able to go back again!"

"But that's what you want! Didn't you say so yourself?" And my father laughed loudly.

"I don't see anything to laugh about."

"Sleep well, little dunce. If we don't hear the put-put of a certain motorcycle at our gates by tomorrow, I shall complain to the district administration."

There was no need to make this complaint. The next day, sure enough, the director's motorcycle drove up to our gate. He came in, and my father, as well as the rest, greeted him amiably: "Good evening, sir."

A chair was offered the guest, and he and my father sat down. At a motion from the latter we withdrew and watched from a distance. Their conversation appeared to be friendly, and evidently it was, for from that time on, my sister and I experienced no further horrors at school.

Yet, for all that, the scandal was not hushed up. A few months later the director was forced to resign because of a petition signed by all of the parents. The rumor had gotten about that he was using some of the students as houseboys for the convenience of his wives. These students had been boarded with him by their parents so that they might receive special attention, and their board had been paid for with cattle. I don't know if anything further came of it. All I know is that it was the straw that broke the camel's back, and that we were never again bullied by the older boys.

SEVEN

I was growing up. The time had come for me to join the society of the uninitiated. This rather mysterious society—and at that age it was very mysterious to me, though not very secret—comprised all the young boys, all the uncircumcised, of twelve, thirteen and fourteen years of age, and it was run by our elders, whom we called the big *Kondéns*. I joined it one evening before the feast of Ramadan.

As soon as the sun had gone down, the tom-tom had begun to beat. Even though it was being played in a remote part of the concession, its notes had roused me at once, had struck my breast, had struck right at my heart, just as if Kodoké, our best player, had been playing for me alone. A little later I had heard the shrill voices of boys accompanying the tom-tom with their cries and singing. Yes, the time had come for me.

It was the first time I had spent the feast of Ramadan at Kouroussa. Until this year, my grandmother had always insisted on my spending it with her at Tindican. All that morning and even more so in the afternoon, I had been in a state of great agitation, with everyone busy preparing for the festival, bumping into and pushing each other and asking me to help. Outside, the uproar was just as bad. Kouroussa is the chief town of our region, and all the canton chiefs, attended by their musicians, make it a custom to gather here for the festival. From the gateway to the concession I had watched them pass by, with their companies of praise-singers, balaphonists and guitarists, drum and tom-tom players. Until now I had only been thinking of the festival and of the sumptuous feast that awaited me—but now there was something quite different in the wind.

The screaming crowd that surrounded Kodoké and his famous tom-tom was getting nearer. Going from one concession to another, the crowd would stop where there was a boy of an age, to join the society, and take him away. That is why it was so slow in coming, yet so sure, so ineluctable. As sure, as ineluctable as the fate that awaited me.

What fate? My meeting with Kondén Diara!

Now I was not unaware of who Kondén Diara was. My mother had often talked of him, and so at times had my uncles and whoever else had authority over me. They had threatened me only too often with Kondén Diara, that terrible bogeyman, that "lion that eats up little boys." And here was Kondén Diara—but was he a man? Was he an animal? Was he not rather half-man, half-animal? My friend Kouyaté believed he was more man than beast—here was Kondén Diara leaving the dim world of hearsay, here he was taking on flesh and blood, yes, and roused by Kodoké's tom-tom was prowling around the town! This night was to be the night of Kondén Diara.

Now I could hear the beating of the tom-tom very plainly —Kodoké was much nearer—I could hear perfectly the chanting and the shouts that rose into the dark. I could make out almost as distinctly the rather hollow, crisp, well-marked beats of the *coros* that are a kind of miniature canoe, and are beaten with a bit of wood. I was standing at the entrance to the concession, waiting. I, too, was holding my *coro*, ready to play it with the stick clutched nervously in my hand. I was waiting, hidden by the shadow of the hut. I was waiting, filled with a dreadful anxiety, my eyes searching the blackness.

"Well?" asked my father.

He had crossed the workshop without my hearing him.

"Are you afraid?"

"A little," I replied.

He laid his hand on my shoulder.

"It's all right. Don't worry."

He drew me to him, and I could feel his warmth; it warmed me, too, and I began to feel less frightened; my heart did not beat so fast.

"You mustn't be afraid."

"No."

I knew that whatever my fear might be I must be brave.

I wasn't to show fright or to run off and hide. Still less was I to resist or cry out when my elders carried me off.

"I, too, went through this test," said my father.

"What happens to you?" I asked.

"Nothing you need really be afraid of, nothing you can not overcome by your own will power. Remember: you have to control your fear; you have to control yourself. Kondén Diara will not take you away. He will roar. But he won't do more than roar. You won't be frightened, now, will you?"

"I'll try not to be."

"Even if you are frightened, do not show it."

He went away, and I began waiting again, and the disturbing uproar came nearer and nearer. Suddenly I saw the crowd emerging from the dark and rushing towards me. Kodoké, his tom-tom slung over one shoulder, was marching at their head, followed by the drummers.

I ran back quickly into the yard, and, standing in the middle of it, I awaited the awful invasion with as much courage as I could manage. I did not have long to wait. The crowd was upon me. It was spreading tumultuously all around me, overwhelming me with shouts and cries and beating tom-toms, beating drums. It formed a circle, and I found myself in the center, alone, curiously isolated, still free and yet already captive. Inside the circle, I recognized Kouyaté and others, many of them friends of mine who had been collected as the crowd moved on, collected as I was to be, as I already was; and it seemed to me they were none of them looking very happy—but was I any more happy than they? I began to beat my *coro*, as they were doing. Perhaps I was beating it with less confidence than they.

At this point young girls and women joined the circle and began to dance; young men and adolescents, stepping out of the crowd, moved into the circle too and began to dance facing the women. The men sang, the women clapped their hands. Soon the only ones left to form the circle were the uncircumcised boys. They too began to sing—they were not allowed to dance—and, as they sang, sang in unison, they forgot their anxiety. I too sang with them. When, having formed a circle again, the crowd left our concession, I went with it, almost willingly, beating my *coro* with great enthusiasm. Kouyaté was on my right.

Toward the middle of the night our tour of the town and the collection of uncircumcised boys were finished. We had arrived at the farthest outskirts of the concessions, and in front of us lay only the brush. Here the women and young girls left us. Then the grown men left. We were alone with the older boys, or should I say "delivered over" to them—for I remember the often rather disagreeable natures and rarely pleasant manners of those older ones.

The women and young girls now hurried back to their dwellings. Actually, they can not have been any more at ease than we were. I know for a fact that not one of them would have ventured to leave town on this night. Already, they found the town and the night sinister. I am certain that more than one who went back to her concession alone was to regret having joined the crowd. They took courage only after they had shut the gates of their concessions and the doors of their huts. Meanwhile, they hurried on and from time to time cast unquiet looks behind them. In a short while, when Kondén Diara would begin to roar, they would not be able to stop shaking with fright; they would all shake uncontrollably. Then they would run to make sure the doors were all properly barred. For them, as for us, though in a much less significant way, this night would be the night of Kondén Diara.

As soon as our elders had made sure that no intruder was present to disturb the mysteriousness of the ceremony, we left the town behind and entered the bush by a path which leads to a sacred place where each year the initiation takes place. The place is well known: it is situated under an enormous bombax tree, a hollow at the junction of the river Komoni and the river Niger. At normal times it is not forbidden to go there; but certainly it has not always been so, and some emanation from the past I never knew still seems to hover around the huge trunk of the bombax tree. I think that a night such as the one we were going through must certainly have resurrected a part of that past.

We were walking in silence, closely hemmed in by our elders. Perhaps they were afraid we might escape? It looked like it. I do not think, however, that the idea of escape had occurred to any of us. The night, and that particular night, seemed impenetrable. Who knew where Kondén Diara had his lair? Who knew where he was prowling? But was it not right here, near the hollow? Yes, it must be here. And if we had to face him—and certainly we had to face him—it would surely be better to do so in a crowd, in this jostling group that seemed to make us all one, and seemed like a last refuge from the peril that was approaching.

Yet for all our nearness to one another and for all the vigilance of our elders, our march—so silent after the recent uproar—through the wan moonlight, far from the town, frightened us. And we were filled with terror at the thought of the sacred place toward which we were going, and the hidden presence of Kondén Diara.

Were our elders marching so closely beside us only to keep watch over us? Perhaps. But it is likely that they too felt something of the terror which had seized us. They too found the night and the silence disturbing. And for them, as for us, marching close together was a means of allaying terror.

Just before we reached the hollow we saw flames leap from a huge wood fire previously hidden by bushes. Kouyaté squeezed my arm, and I knew he was referring to the fire. Yes, there was a fire. There too was Kondén Diara, the hidden presence of Kondén Diara. But there was also a reassuring presence in the depth of the night: a great fire! My spirits rose—at least they rose a little—and I squeezed Kouyaté's arm in return. I quickened my steps—we all quickened our steps —and the crimson radiance of the fire enveloped us. We had a harbor now, this kind of haven from the night: a huge blaze, and, at our backs, the enormous trunk of the bombax tree. Oh! It was a precarious haven! But, however poor, it was infinitely better than the silence and the dark, the sullen silence of the dark. We assembled beneath the bombax tree. The ground beneath had been cleared of reeds and tall grasses.

Our elders suddenly shouted: "Kneel!"

We at once fell to our knees.

"Heads down!"

We lowered our heads.

"Lower than that!"

We bent our heads right to the ground, as if in prayer.

"Now hide your eyes!"

We didn't have to be told twice. We shut our eyes tight and pressed our hands over them. For would we not die of fright and horror if we should see, or so much as catch a glimpse of the Kondén Diara? Our elders walked up and down, behind us and in front of us, to make sure that we had all obeyed their orders to the letter. Woe to him who would have the audacity to disobey! He would be cruelly whipped. It would be a whipping all the more cruel because he would have no hope of redress, for he would find no one to listen to his complaint, no one to transgress against custom. But who would have the audacity to disobey?

Now that we were on our knees with our foreheads to the ground and our hands pressed over our eyes, Kondén Diara's roaring suddenly burst out.

We were expecting to hear this hoarse roar, we were not expecting any other sound, but it took us by surprise and shattered us, froze our hearts with its unexpectedness. And it was not only a lion, it was not only Kondén Diara roaring: there were ten, twenty, perhaps thirty lions that took their lead fom him, uttering their terrible roars and surrounding the hollow; ten or twenty lions separated from us by a few yards only and whom the great wood fire would perhaps not always keep at bay; lions of every size and every age—we could tell that by the way they roared—from the very oldest ones to the very youngest cubs. No, not one of us would dream of venturing to open an eye, not one! Not one of us would dare to lift his head from the ground; he would rather bury it in the earth. And I bent down as far as I could; we all bent down further; we bent our knees as much as we

could; we kept our backs as low as possible. I made myself—
we all made ourselves—as small as we could.

"You mustn't be afraid!" I said to myself. "You must
master your fear! Your father has commanded you to!"

But how was I to master it? Even in the town, far away
from this clearing, women and children trembled and hid
themselves in their huts. They heard the growling of Kondén
Diara, and many of them stopped their ears to keep it out.
The braver arose—that night it took courage to leave one's
bed—and went again and again to check the doors and see
that they were shut tight. How was I to stave off fear when
I was within range of the dread monster? If he pleased,
Kondén Diara could leap the fire in one bound and sink his
claws in my back!

I did not doubt the presence of the monster, not for a
single instant. Who could assemble such a numerous herd,
hold such a nocturnal revel, if not Kondén Diara?

"He alone," I said to myself, "he alone has such power
over lions. . . . Keep away, Kondén Diara! Keep away! Go
back into the bush! . . ." But Kondén Diara went on with
his revels, and sometimes it seemed to me that he roared right
over my head, right into my own ears. "Keep away, I im-
plore you, Kondén Diara!"

What was it my father had said? "Kondén Diara roars;
but he won't do more than roar; he will not take you away
. . ." Yes, something like that. But was it true, really true?

There was also a rumor that Kondén Diara sometimes
pounced with fearsome claws on someone or other and carried him far away, far, far away into the depths of the bush;
and then, days and days afterwards, months or even years

later, quite by chance a huntsman might discover some whitened bones.

And do not people also die of fright? Ah! how I wished this roaring would stop! How I wished I was far away from this clearing, back in the concession, in the warm security of the hut! Would this roaring never cease?

"Go away, Kondén Diara! Go away! Stop roaring." Oh! those roars! I felt as if I could bear them no longer.

Whereupon, suddenly, they stopped! They stopped just as they had begun, so suddenly, in fact, that I felt only reluctant relief. Was it over? Really over? Was it not just a temporary interruption? No, I dared not feel relieved just yet. And then suddenly the voice of one of the older boys rang out: "Get up!"

I heaved a sigh of relief. This time it was really over. We looked at one another: I looked at Kouyaté and the others. If there were only a little more light. . . . But the light from the fire was sufficient: great drops of sweat were still beading our foreheads; yet the night was chill. . . . Yes, we were afraid. We were not able to conceal our fear.

A new command rang out, and we sat down in front of the fire. Now our elders began our initiation. For the rest of the night they taught us the chants sung by the uncircumcised. We never moved. We learned the words and tunes as we heard them. We were attentive as if we had been at school, entirely attentive and docile.

When dawn came, our instruction was at an end. My legs and arms were numb. I worked my joints and rubbed my legs for a while, but my blood still flowed slowly. I was worn out, and I was cold. Looking around me, I could not understand why I had shaken with fear during the night: the first rays of dawn were falling so gently, so reassuringly, on the bombax tree, on the clearing. The sky looked so pure! Who would have believed that a few hours earlier a pack of lions led by Kondén Diara in person had been raging fiercely in the high grass and among the reeds, and that they had been separated from us only by a wood fire which had just now gone out as dawn came? No one. I would have doubted my own senses and set it all down as a nightmare if I had not noticed more than one of my companions casting an occasional fearful glance in the direction of the highest grass.

But what were those long white threads which hung from, or, rather, waved from the top of the bombax tree and which appeared to write on the sky the direction in which the town lay? I had not time to wonder very long at this: our elders were regrouping us; and, because most of us were almost sleep-walking, the operation was carried out with difficulty, with shouts, and with some rough treatment. Finally we started off back to the town, singing our new songs, and we sang them with unbelievably carefree abandon: as the steed that scents the approaching stable suddenly quickens his step, however weary he may be.

When we reached the first concessions, the presence of the long white threads struck me once more: all the principal huts had these threads on the very tops of their roofs.

"Do you see the white threads?" I asked Kouyaté.

"I can see them. They are always there after the ceremony in the clearing."

"Who puts them there?"

Kouyaté shrugged his shoulders.

"That's where they come from," I said, pointing to the distant bombax tree.

"Someone must have climbed up."

"Who could possibly climb a bombax tree?"

"I don't know."

"Could anyone possibly get his arms around such a huge trunk?" I said. "And even if he could, how could he hoist himself on bark all covered with all those thorns? You're talking nonsense. Can't you imagine what a job it would be just to reach the first branches?"

"Why do you expect me to know more about this than you do?" asked Kouyaté.

"Because this is the first time I have taken part in the ceremony, while you—"

I didn't finish my sentence. We had reached the main square of the town. I stared in amazement at the bombax trees in the market place. They too were ornamented with the same white threads. All but the humblest huts, indeed, and all the big trees were tied to one another by these white threads whose focal point was the enormous bombax tree in the clearing, the sacred place marked by the bombax tree.

"The swallows tie them on," said Kouyaté suddenly.

"Swallows? Are you crazy?" I said. "Swallows don't fly by night."

I questioned one of the older boys who was walking beside me.

"It is our great chief who does it," he said. "Our chief turns himself into a swallow during the night. He flies from tree to tree and from hut to hut, and all these threads are tied on in less time than it takes to tell."

"He flies from tree to tree like a swallow?"

"Yes. He's a real swallow and as swift. Everyone knows that."

"Isn't that what I told you?" asked Kouyaté.

I did not say another word. The night of Kondén Diara was a strange night, a terrible and miraculous night, a night that passed all understanding.

As on the previous evening, we went from one concession to another, preceded by tom-toms and drums, and our companions left us one after another as they reached their homes. Whenever we passed a concession where someone whose courage had failed him had refused to join us, a mocking chant rose from our ranks.

I arrived at our concession completely exhausted but very satisfied with myself: I had taken part in the ceremony of the lions! Even if I had not put up much of a show when Kondén Diara was roaring, that was my own affair; I could keep that to myself. I passed triumphantly over the threshold of our concession.

The festival of Ramadan was beginning. In the yard, I saw my parents, who were dressed to go to the mosque.

"Here you are at last," said my mother.

"Here I am," I said proudly.

"What kind of time is this to come home?" she said, pressing me to her bosom. "The night is over, and you haven't had a bit of sleep."

"The ceremony did not finish until break of day," I said.

"I know, I know," she said. "All you men are mad."

"What about the lions?" asked my father. "What about Kondén Diara?"

"I heard them," I replied. "They were very close; they were as near to me as I am to you now. There was only the fire between us."

"It's crazy," said my mother. "Go to bed, you're dropping with sleep." She turned toward my father: "Now, where's the sense in all that?"

"Well, it's the custom," said my father.

"I don't like such customs," she said. "Young boys should not have to stay awake all night."

"Were you afraid?" asked my father.

Should I admit that I was very frightened?

"Of course he was afraid," said my mother.

"Only a little," said my father.

"Go to bed," ordered my mother. "If you don't get some sleep now you'll fall asleep during the feast."

I went inside to lie down. Outside I heard my mother quarreling with my father. She thought it stupid to take unnecessary risks.

Later I got to know who Kondén Diara was, and I learned these things when the time had come for me to learn them. As long as we are not circumcised, as long as we have not attained that second life that is our true existence, we are told nothing, and we can find out nothing.

We begin to have a vague understanding of the ceremony of the lions after we have taken part in it many times. But even then, we are careful to share our knowledge only with those companions who have had the same experience. And the real secret lies hidden until the day when we are initiated into our life as men.

No, they were not real lions that roared in the clearing,

for it was the older boys, simply the older boys. They created
the roaring sound with small boards, thick at the center,
sharp at the edges: the edges were all sharper from having
such a thick center. The board was ellipsoidal in shape and
very small. There was a hole on one side that permitted it
to be tied to a string. The older boys swung it around like
a sling, and, to increase the speed of the gyrations, they
too turned with it. The board cut through the air and produced a sound like a lion's roar. The smallest boards imi-
tated the roaring of the lion cubs; the biggest ones the roaring of full-grown lions.

It was childishly simple. What was not so childish was
the effect produced at night on someone who did not expect
it: the heart froze! If it had not been for the far greater fear
of finding themselves lost in the bush, the terror it created
would have made the boys run away. The bombax tree and
the fire which had been kindled near it made a kind of haven
which kept the uninitiated from running away.

But if Kondén Diara's roaring is easily explained, the
presence of the long white threads binding the great bombax
tree in the sacred clearing, to the tallest trees and the principal houses of the town, is less easily explained. For my own
part, I never succeeded in obtaining an explanation: at the
time when I might have obtained it, that is, when I should
have taken my place among the older boys who conducted
the ceremony, I was no longer living at Kouroussa. All I
know is that these threads were spun from cotton and that
bamboo poles were used to tie them to the tops of the huts.
What I don't know is how they were attached to the tops
of the bombax trees.

Our bombax trees are very big, and it is difficult to imagine poles sixty feet high. Such structures would certainly collapse, no matter how carefully they had been put together. Moreover, I do not see how the summit of these thorny trees could be reached by climbing. There is of course a kind of belt which tree-climbers use. It is tied around the tree and the climber gets inside it, placing the belt against the small of his back, then climbs by a series of jerks, pressing against the trunk with his feet. But such a procedure is quite preposterous given the enormous size of the trunks of our bombax trees.

Or why not plainly and simply use a sling? I do not know. A good slinger can work miracles. Perhaps it is this sort of miracle which would most easily explain the inexplicable presence of white threads at the summit of the bombax trees. But I can come to no final decision about it.

I do know that the men who tie the threads to the rooftops have to take great care not to mislay the bamboo poles. Things must not be revealed in that fashion. For it would take only one mislaid pole to start the women and children on the way to discovering the secret. That is why, as soon as the threads are tied, the poles and boards are removed. The usual hideouts are thatched roofs and secret places in the bush. And so nothing escapes about these manifestations of the power of Kondén Diara.

But what about the men? What about those who *do* know?

They won't breathe a single word about it. They keep their knowledge a close secret. Not only do they keep women and children in a state of uncertainty and terror, they also warn them to keep the doors of their huts firmly barred.

I know that such conduct must appear strange, but it is absolutely true. If the ceremony of the lions has the character of a game, if it is for the most part pure mystification, yet it has one important feature: it is a test, a training in hardship, a rite; the prelude to a tribal rite, and for the present that is all one can say. . . . It is obvious that if the secret were to be given away, the ceremony would lose much of its power. Certainly the teaching which follows the roaring of Kondén Diara would remain the same. But nothing would remain of the trial by fear, that occasion when every boy has the opportunity to overcome his fear and his own baser nature. Nothing would remain of the necessary preparation for the painful tribal rite of circumcision. But, at the moment of writing this, does any part of the rite still survive? The secret. . . . Do we still have secrets?

EIGHT

Later on, I went through an ordeal much more frightening than Kondén Diara, a really dangerous ordeal, and no game: circumcision.

I was in my final year of school. I was at last one of the big boys who used to bully us when we were in the beginners' class. Fortunately the hardships we had endured then had since been abolished.

But it was not enough to be in the upper class. We had to be mature in every sense of the word; we had to become men.

Now, I had always been a child. I was thought to be immature, a baby among my classmates, most of whom had been circumcised. I believe I *was* somewhat younger than they. It may have been that my many visits to Tindican had delayed my initiation. Whatever the facts, I was now at the age when I too must be reborn, must give up childhood and become a man.

I approached this transition to manhood apprehensively. The thought of it greatly disturbed me. Of course the ceremony itself, at least the visible part of it, was familiar to every candidate, for each year we had watched the novices dancing in the main square of the town. But the essential part of the ceremony remained a secret, and we only had a vague notion of how it was performed, though we did know that the operation would be painful.

The public and private ceremonies differ completely. The former is an occasion for rejoicing, for a great and very noisy festival in which the whole town participates and which lasts for several days. It is almost as if the noise and activity and dancing and merry-making were contrived to make us forget the approaching ordeal. But our anxiety was not so easily dispelled. The pain of the operation was always in our minds.

This festival was unlike others. Although it was supposed to be entirely joyful, there was a gravity about it that other festivals did not have, a gravity arising from the fact that the event which it commemorated was the most important event in life: to be exact, the beginning of a new life. Despite the noise and movement, the flowing rhythms and the whirling dance, we were ever conscious of the test, the mysterious secret rite.

But, however great the anxiety, however certain the pain, no one would have dreamed of running away from the ordeal —no more than one would have dreamed of running away from the ordeal of the lions—and I, for my own part, never entertained such thoughts. I wanted to be born, to be born again. I knew perfectly well that I was going to be hurt, but I wanted to be a man, and it seemed to me that nothing could be too painful if, by enduring it, I was to come to man's estate. My companions felt the same. Like me, they were prepared to pay for it with their blood. Our elders before us had paid for it thus; those who were born after us would pay for it in their turn. Why should we be spared? Life itself would spring from the shedding of our blood.

That year, in the main square at Kouroussa, I danced for a whole week the dance of the *soli*, which is the dance of those who are to be circumcised. Every afternoon my companions and I would go to the dancing-place, wearing a cap and a *boubou* which reached to our heels, a much longer *boubou* than is generally worn, and split up the sides; the cap, a skull-cap, was decorated with a pompom that hung down at the back; and this was our first man's hat. The women and girls would come running to the gates of their concessions to watch us go by. Then they followed closely on our heels, decked in their holiday finery. The tom-tom throbbed, and we danced in the square until we were ready to drop. And, as the week wore on, the dances grew longer and the crowds larger.

My *boubou*, like that of my companions, was of a brownish-red color, a color on which bloodstains would not show too clearly. It had been specially woven for the ceremony, and had first of all been white; the masters of the ceremonies had then dyed it with dyes made from the bark of trees, after which they had plunged it into the muddy water of a pool in the brush. In order that it might take on the desired tone, the *boubou* had been left to soak for several weeks, perhaps because of some ritual reason which I have forgotten. The cap, apart from the pompom which remained white, had been treated in the same fashion.

We would dance until we were out of breath; but we were not the only ones dancing: the whole town danced with us! They came in throngs to watch. The whole town came, because the test, so very important to us, was equally important to all. No one could be indifferent to the fact that this second birth, our real birth, would increase the population of the town by a new group of citizens. In our country, all dances have a cumulative tendency, because each beat of the tom-tom has an almost irresistible appeal. Soon, those who were just spectators would dance too. They would crowd into the open space, and, though they did not mix with our group, they would take an intimate part in our revels, rivaling us in their frenzy, men as well as women, women as well as girls, though the women and girls danced apart from us.

While I was dancing, my *boubou,* split from top to bottom at each side, would reveal a great piece of the brightly colored silk handkerchief which I had knotted around my loins. I was quite aware of this, and did nothing to prevent it. In fact, I did all I could to show it off. This was because we each wore a similar handkerchief, more or less colorful, more or less ornate, which we had received from our acknowledged sweetheart. She would make us a present of it for the ceremony, and it was generally taken from her own head. As the handkerchief can not pass unnoticed, as it is the one personal note that distinguishes the common uniform, and, as its design, like its color, makes it easy to identify, the wearing of it is a kind of public manifestation of a relationship— a purely childlike relationship, it goes without saying—which the present ceremony may break forever, or, as the case may be, transform into something less innocent and more lasting. Now, if our so-called sweetheart was in the least pretty and consequently desirable, we would swing our hips with great abandon, to make our *boubous* fly more freely from side to side, and thus show off our handkerchiefs to greater advantage. At the same time we kept our ears open to catch anything that might be said about us, about our sweetheart, and about our good fortune. But our ears caught very little, for the music was deafening; and there was extraordinary animation in the tightly packed crowds all around the square.

From time to time, a man would break through the crowd and come toward us. It would generally be an older man, often a person of some consequence, who was on friendly terms with, or had obligations toward, one of our families. The man would indicate that he wished to speak, the tom-toms would stop, and the dancing would be interrupted for a moment. We would gather around him. Thereupon, the man would address himself to one or the other of us in a very loud voice.

"O thou!" he would say, "Hearken unto me. Thy family has always been beloved of my family; thy grandfather is the friend of my father, thy father is my friend, and thou art the friend of my son. I come here this day that I may testify these things in public. Let every man here know that we are friends, and that we shall ever remain so. And as a symbol of this lasting friendship, and in order to show my gratitude for the good will that thy father and thy grandfather have always shown to me and mine, I make thee this gift of an ox on the occasion of thy circumcision."

We would all applaud him; the entire assembly would applaud him. Many of the older men, all of them friends indeed, came forward like this and made an announcement of what gifts they were going to present. Each one made an offering in accordance with his means, and in the spirit of rivalry often made it beyond his means. If it was not an ox, it would be sack of rice, or millet or maize.

For the great feast of the circumcision is the occasion of a great banquet attended by numerous guests; a banquet so enormous that, despite the number of guests, there is enough to eat for days and days before the end is reached. Obviously, this entails great expense. So whoever is a friend of the family of the boy to be circumcised, or is bound to the family by bonds of obligation, makes it a point of honor to contribute to the banquet; and he will help those who are in need of help and those who are not. That is why, at each circumcision, there is this sudden abundance of gifts and good things.

Did we enjoy this sudden shower of gifts? Not unreservedly. The ordeal that awaited us was not of the kind that whets the appetite. No, we would not be likely to have much appetite, when, the circumcision over, we were invited to take part in the banquet. Though we did not know it by actual experience, we were quite well aware that freshly circumcised boys have a rather woebegone look.

This reflection would brutally recall our fears: we would be applauding the donor, and at the same time our thoughts would be returning to the ordeal before us. As I have said: this apprehension in the midst of the general excitement, an excitement in which we, through our constant dancing, took a major part, was not the least paradoxical aspect of those days. Were we not dancing to forget what we were all dreading? I can quite believe it. And in truth there were moments when we succeeded in forgetting it. But anxiety was never far away. There were always fresh occasions for it to spring to life again. Our mothers might make increased sacrifices on our behalf—and certainly they did not fail to do so—yet they were but sorry comfort.

Sometimes one of our mothers, or some other close relative, would join the dance, and often in dancing she would wave aloft the symbol of our class. It was generally a hoe—the peasant class in Guinea is by far the most numerous—and this was to show that the boy who was about to be circumcised was a good laborer.

This was when I saw my father's second wife make her appearance holding aloft an exercise book and a fountain pen. I must confess that this gave me no pleasure at all, and, rather than encouraging me, it somewhat embarrassed me, although I knew quite well that my second mother was merely observing an old custom, and doing so with the best will in the world, since the exercise book and the fountain pen were the symbols of a profession which, in her eyes, was superior to that of a farmer or a mechanic.

My real mother was infinitely more discreet: she simply watched me from a distance. I even noticed that she tried to hide in the crowd. I am sure she was at least as anxious as I was, though she took the greatest trouble to conceal the fact. But, for the most part, the excitement was such, so all pervasive, that we had to bear the burden of our uneasiness ourselves.

Need I mention that we ate rapidly and without relish? It goes without saying: everything centered on the dancing, and on the preparations for the feast. We would go home footsore and weary, and sleep like stones. In the morning we could never get up, but lay in bed until the very last moment, when the tom-tom began to summon us. What did it matter if we had no proper meals? We barely had time to eat. We had to wash at top speed, fling on our *boubous*, jam our caps on our heads, run to the main square and dance. And each day we had to dance more. For we were all dancing now, the whole town was dancing, afternoon and evening— by torchlight in the evening—and on the eve of the ordeal, the town danced all day and all night.

On this final day, we were all worked up into a kind of strange excitement. The men who perform this initiation, after having shaved their heads, gathered us together in a hut built apart from the concessions. This hut, which was very spacious, would henceforward be our dwelling place. The spacious square in which it stood was fenced off by such tightly woven reeds that no inquisitive eyes could see through them.

When we entered the hut, we saw our *boubous* and caps spread on the ground. During the night, our *boubous* had been stitched up the sides except for the armholes, so that they covered us completely. As for the caps, they had been transformed into tremendously high bonnets. The material, which had originally hung loose, had been stiffened by fixing it to a wicker framework. We slipped into our *boubous*, which made us look rather as if we were in tight sheaths; and now we looked even skinnier than we really were. Then, when we had put on our long, narrow bonnets, we looked at each other for a moment. In any other circumstances we would certainly have burst out laughing: we looked as long and as thin as bamboo poles.

"Go and walk outside for a while," the men told us. "You must get used to having your *boubous* sewed up."

We took a little walk; but we could not take large strides, for the stitched-up *boubous* prevented that. The cloth held firm and our legs knocked against it. It was as if we were in shackles.

We came back to the hut, sat down on the mats, and remained there under the supervision of the men. We chattered among ourselves of one thing and another, concealing our uneasiness as best we could. But how could we banish from our minds the thought of tomorrow's ceremony? Our uneasiness was apparent, underlying all our chatter. The men who were with us were aware of our state of mind. Whenever, in spite of ourselves, we gave way to our anxiety, they were at great pains to reassure us. In this respect, they were quite different from the big boys who had performed the ceremony of the lions and who had wanted only to frighten us as much as possible.

"Come, don't be afraid," they said. "This has happened

to all men. Has it done them any harm? It won't do you any harm either. Now that you are going to become men, conduct yourselves like men; drive away your fears. A man is afraid of nothing."

But we were still children. All through that final day, and all through that final night, we would remain children. As I have said before, we were not even supposed to have reached the age of discretion. And if that age is a long time in coming, if it really comes only after many years, our "manhood" would seem all the more premature. We were still children. Tomorrow . . . but it was better to think of something else; to think, for example, of the whole town gathered in the main square, happily dancing. But what about us? Were not we, too, about to join the dance?

No. This time we were going to dance on our own. We were going to dance, and the others were going to watch. At present we were not allowed to mix with other people. Our mothers could not even speak to, let alone touch, us. We left the hut, swathed in our long sheaths, and with our enormous bonnets towering on our heads.

As soon as we appeared in the main square, the men ran to meet us. We advanced single file between two rows of men. Kouyaté's father, a venerable old man with white beard and white hair, thrust through the ranks and placed himself at our head. It was his privilege to show us how to dance the *coba*, a dance kept, like the *soli*, for those who are about to be circumcised and which is danced only on the eve of circumcision. Kouyaté's father, by virtue of his great age and good name, was the only one who had the right to strike up the chant which accompanies the *coba*.

I walked behind him. He told me to put my hands on his shoulders, and then each of us placed his hands on the shoulders of the boy in front of him. When our single file had been linked up in this way, the tom-toms and drums suddenly ceased, and everyone was silent, everything became silent and still Kouyaté's father then drew himself up to his full height, cast his eyes all around him—there was something imperious and noble in his attitude—and, as if it were a command, lifted up his voice in the *coba* chant:

"*Coba! Aye coba, lama!*"

At once the tom-toms and the drums shattered the silence and we all took up the phrase:

"*Coba! Aye coba, lama!*"

We were walking like Kouyaté's father, legs as far apart as our *boubous* would allow, and naturally with very slow steps. As we chanted the words, we turned our heads, like Kouyaté's father, to the left, and then to the right; and our high bonnets extended this head movement in a curious way.

"*Coba! Aye coba, lama!*"

We began to march around the square. The men fell back as we approached, and, when the last of us had passed by, regrouped themselves a little further on, and once again fell back to make room for us. Because we marched slowly and with our legs wide apart, our march had a somewhat burlesque air.

"*Coba! Aye coba, lama!*"

The two ranks of men through which we were moving were thick and tightly packed. The women behind could scarcely see more than our high bonnets, and the children, obviously even less than that. In previous years, I had caught only glimpses of the tops of the bonnets. But it was enough: the *coba* is a man's affair. The women. . . . No, the women had no voice in this matter.

"*Coba! Aye coba, lama!*"

Finally, we reached the spot where we had begun our dance. Then Kouyaté's father stopped, the tom-toms and drums fell silent, and we went back to our hut. We had barely left the square before the dancing and shouting began again.

Three times that day, we appeared in the main square to dance the *coba*; and three times again during the night, by torchlight. Each time, the men enclosed us in a living hedge. We did not get any sleep. No one went to bed. The whole town stayed awake and danced all through the night. As we left our hut for the sixth time, dawn was breaking.

"*Coba! Aye coba, lama!*"

Our bonnets still moved in time to the rhythm, our *boubous* were still stretched over our straddling legs. But we were beginning to flag, our eyes were burning feverishly, and our anxiety was mounting. If we had not been urged on, carried away by the tom-tom beat. . . . But it urged us, carried us away! And we danced on obediently, our heads curiously light from lack of sleep, curiously heavy too, with thoughts of the fate that was to be ours.

"*Coba! Aye coba, lama!*"

As we came to the end of the dance, dawn began to lighten the main square. This time we did not go back to our hut. We went immediately into the bush. We went a long way, to where there was no risk of our being disturbed. In the main square the dancing had stopped. The people had all gone home. Nevertheless, a few men followed us out. The rest awaited in their huts the ceremonial shots that would announce to all that one more man, one more Malinké, had been born.

We reached a circular clearing where the ground was completely bare. All around, grasses grew high, higher than the men's heads. It was the most secluded spot one could have found. We were lined up, each of us in front of a stone. At the other end of the clearing the men stood facing us. And we took off our clothes.

I was afraid, terribly afraid, and I needed all my will power not to show it. All those men standing in front of us and watching us must see nothing of my fear. My companions showed themselves as brave as I, and it was absolutely necessary that it should be so. Perhaps a future father-in-law or a future relative was among those men standing in front of us. We dared not let ourselves down now!

Suddenly the operator appeared. We had caught a glimpse of him the night before, when he had performed his dance in the main square. And now too I only caught a brief glimpse of him. I had hardly realized he was there before I saw him standing in front of me.

Was I afraid? I mean, was I even more afraid, had I at that particular moment a fresh access of fear—for I had been beset by fears ever since I had entered the clearing? I did not have time to be afraid. I felt something like a burn and I closed my eyes for the fraction of a second. I do not think I cried out. No, I can not have cried out. I certainly did not have time to do that either. When I opened my eyes the operator was bent over my neighbor. In a few seconds that year's dozen or so boys had become men. The operator made me pass from one state to the other with an indescribable rapidity.

Later, I learned that he was of the Daman family, my mother's family. He had a great reputation, and rightly so, for at the most important festivals he had often circumcised several hundreds of boys in less than an hour. This rapidity was very much appreciated, for it did not prolong the agony. Therefore, all parents who could, had recourse to him, since he was the most skillful. He would be their guest for the evening, and the guest of the most important men in the town. Then he would go back to his hut in the country.

As soon as the operation was over, the guns were fired. Our mothers and our relatives in the concessions heard the reports. And while we were forced to sit on the stone in front of us, messengers rushed away and tore through the bush to announce the happy news. They arrived bathed in sweat and gasping for breath, so much so, that they could hardly deliver their message to the families that came running to meet them.

"Truly your son has been very brave," they would shout to the mother of the circumcised boy.

And indeed we had all been very brave. We had all concealed our fear very carefully. But now perhaps we were not quite so brave, for the hemorrhage that follows the operation is abundant, very long and disturbing. All that blood lost! I watched my blood flowing away, and my heart contracted. I thought: "Is my body going to be entirely emptied?" And I raised imploring eyes to our healer, the séma.

"The blood must flow," said the *séma*. "If it did not flow. . . ."

He did not finish the sentence. He was looking at the wound. When he saw that the blood was finally beginning to flow a little less freely, he put on the first bandage. Then he went on to the others.

When the blood had finally ceased flowing we were dressed in our long *boubous* again. Apart from a very brief undershirt, this was to be the only article of attire during the weeks of convalescence that were to come. We stood up awkwardly, lightheaded and sick at our stomachs. Among the men who had been present at the operation I saw several who, taking pity on our plight, turned their heads away to hide their tears.

In the town, our parents were making a fuss over the messenger, and loading him with gifts. The celebration began again. Wasn't it an occasion for rejoicing over the fortunate outcome of our ordeal, for rejoicing over our new birth? Already friends and neighbors were crowding inside the concessions where the newly circumcised lived, and they were beginning to dance the *fady fady*, the dance of manhood, in our honor, until the enormous banquet would be served.

We too were naturally to receive a large share of the feast. The young men who had conducted the ceremony, and who were also our attendants, as well as our supervisors, went to seek our share.

Alas! We had seen and lost too much blood—its unsavory smell still seemed to linger in our nostrils—and we all had a touch of fever. We were shaking. We could cast only sour looks on the succulent dishes. They did not tempt us at all, but filled us with revulsion. Of all that great abundance of food cooked for our enjoyment, we pecked with a ridiculously feeble appetite at only one or two dishes. We sat looking at them, sniffing their savory smells. We would take a mouthful and then turn our heads away. This went on for several days, until the others had consumed all that abundance and the daily menu had been resumed.

At nightfall we took the road back to the town, escorted by the young men and by our healer. We walked with great care. We could not let the *boubou* rub against the wound. But sometimes, in spite of our precautions, it would do so, making us cry out with pain. We would stop for a moment, our faces drawn with suffering. The young men held us up. It took us a very long time to get back to our hut. When we finally reached it we were at the end of our endurance. We lay down at once on our mats.

We waited for sleep, but it was long in coming, for our fever kept us awake. Our eyes wandered miserably over the walls of the hut. At the thought of living here until our period of convalescence was over—several weeks—in the company of these young men and our healer, we were seized with despair. Men! Yes, we were men at last, but what a price to pay! . . . At last we fell asleep. By the next morning our fever had abated, and we were able to laugh at the gloomy thoughts of the night before.

Certainly, the life we led in the hut was not the same as the life we had led in the concessions. But it was not insupportable, and it had its own delights, even though there was constant supervision and the discipline was rather strict. Still, it was wise and reasonable, and its sole aim was to shield us from anything that might retard our convalescence. If we were watched closely day and night, and even more closely at night than during the day, it was because we were allowed to lie neither on our sides nor on our faces. As long as our wounds were not properly healed, we could lie only on our backs and, of course, we were absolutely forbidden to cross our legs. It goes without saying that when we were asleep it was difficult to remain constantly in one position; but if we so much as stirred, the young men were on hand at once to shift our positions, as gently as they could so as not to disturb our rest. They watched over us in relays, so that we never for one second escaped their vigilant eyes.

But perhaps it would be better if I talked about their "attendance" rather than their "supervision." They were more like nurses than supervisors. By day, when, weary of continually lying or sitting on our mats, we asked to be allowed to get up, they would help us. Indeed, at every step we took, they were at our sides supporting us. They brought us our meals; they took news of us to our parents, and brought us news of them. Their task was no easy one. We accepted their good nature, and at times took advantage of it; but they never grumbled. They looked after us with boundless good will.

Our healer was not so indulgent. No doubt he gave us the utmost devotion in his attendance upon us, but he was something of a disciplinarian, though not a harsh one. But he did not like us to make faces when he was cleaning a wound.

"You are not little boys now," he would tell us. "Control yourselves."

And we just had to control ourselves if we did not want to be called hopeless little snivellers. So twice a day we braced ourselves, for our healer used to clean our wounds mornings and evenings. He used water in which certain kinds of bark had been steeping, and as he cleaned the wounds he intoned healing incantations. The task of teaching and initiating us also fell on him.

After the first week, which was passed entirely in the solitude of the hut and whose monotony had been broken by only a few visits from my father, we were able to go for short walks in the bush escorted by our healer.

As long as we remained in the immediate vicinity of the town the young men walked in front. They acted as scouts, so that if some woman was walking in our direction they could warn her in time of our approach and she could go another way. Indeed, we were not supposed to meet any woman at all, not even our own mothers, until our wounds had properly healed. The rule is enforced simply to avoid any delay in the healing. I do not think any other explanation need be sought.

The teaching we received in the bush, far from all prying eyes, had nothing very mysterious about it; nothing, I think, that was not fit for ears other than our own. These lessons, the same as had been taught to all who had preceded us, confined themselves to outlining what a man's conduct should be: we were to be absolutely straightforward, to cultivate all the virtues that go to make an honest man, to fulfill our duties toward God, toward our parents, our superiors and our neighbors. We must tell nothing of what we learned, either to women or to the uninitiated; neither were we to reveal any of the secret rites of circumcision. That is the custom. Women, too, are not allowed to tell anything about the rites of excision.

Should a non-initiate attempt later on to find out what we had been taught and try to pass himself off as an initiate in order to do so, we were told how to expose him. The simplest though not the least laborious device was to use phrases with refrains that had to be whistled in a certain way. There are very many of these, so many that, should the impostor by some extraordinary chance have learned two or three, he will find himself baffled by the fourth or the tenth, if not by the twentieth. Always lengthy, always complicated, it is impossible to imitate these refrains unless they have been whistled time and time again and patiently learned by heart.

They really require very patient study and an alert memory if one is to retain them all, as we finally realized. Whenever our healer thought we were not learning them fast enough—and indeed we were not always very attentive— he would remind us sharply of our duty. He would use the pompoms in our caps to belabor our backs. That would not hurt very much, you may say; but if the pompom is a large one, bound tightly with cotton and with something hard inside, it can be very painful.

By the third week I was allowed to see my mother. When one of the younger men came and said she was at the door, I leaped to my feet.

"Here, not so fast," he said, taking me by the hand. "Wait for me."

"All right, but hurry."

Three weeks! We had never been separated from each other for so long. When I went for the holidays to Tindican I seldom stayed away longer than ten or fifteen days, and that was not to be compared with the length of our present separation.

"Well, are you coming?" I cried.

I quivered with impatience.

"Listen," said the young man. "Listen first of all to what I have to say. You are going to see your mother, you are allowed to see her; but you must stand inside the fence when you speak to her; you must not go beyond the fence!"

"I'll stay inside," I said. "Just let me go."

And I tried to shake off his hand.

"We'll go together," he said.

He had not let go. We left the hut together. The gate in the fence was open. Several of the young men were sitting on the threshold. They signaled to me not to cross it. I bounded over the few yards that separated me from the gate and suddenly I saw my mother. She was standing in the dusty road a few steps away from the fence. She too was forbidden to come any closer.

"Mother!" I cried. "Mother!"

And all at once I felt a lump in my throat. Was it because I could go no closer, because I could not hug my mother? Was it because I had already been separated too long, because we were still to be separated a long time? I do not know. All I know is that I could only say, "Mother!" and that after my joy in seeing her I suddenly felt a strange depression.

Ought I to attribute this emotional instability to the transformation that had been worked in me? When I had left her I was still a child. Now. . . . But was I really a man now? Was I already a grown man? . . . I *was* a man! Yes, I was a grown man. And now this manhood had already begun to stand between my mother and myself. It kept us infinitely further apart than the few yards that separated us.

"Mother!" I said again.

But this time I spoke very low, as if lamenting sadly, as if it were a lament for myself.

"Yes, here I am," she said. "I've come to see you."

"Yes, you've come to see me."

And suddenly I passed from sadness to joy. What was I worrying about? My mother was there. She was here in front of me. I had only to go a couple of steps to be at her side. I would certainly have done so if there had not been that absurd order forbidding me to go beyond the gate.

"I am glad to see you," she went on.

She smiled. At once I understood why she was smiling. When she came she had been a little uneasy, vaguely uneasy. Even though she had had news of my progress, even though my father himself had taken her news of me, and good news, nevertheless she had remained a little uneasy. How did she know that she was being told the truth? But now that she had been to see for herself, she was able to judge that my convalescence was well under way, and she was really glad.

"I am really very glad," she said.

But she said nothing more. This casual reference was enough. One must not speak openly of anyone's return to health, especially ours. That would not be wise. It would be tempting hostile spirits to attack us.

"I brought you some *cola* nuts," she said.

And she opened the little basket she held in her hand and showed me the nuts. One of the young men who was sitting by the gate went and took them and gave them to me.

"Thank you, Mother."

"Now I must be getting home."

"Say goodbye for me to my father, and to everyone."

"Yes, I shall do so."

"It won't be long now, Mother."

"Not very long."

Her voice was trembling a little. I went in at once. Our meeting had not lasted two minutes, but that was all we were allowed. And all the time there had been that unbreachable space between us. Poor mother! She had not even held me in her arms. However, I am sure she walked away, as she always did, with great dignity. She had always held herself very erect, and that made her appear taller than she was. I visualized her walking along the dusty road, her dress falling in noble folds, her waistband neatly tied, and her hair carefully plaited and drawn back at the nape of her neck. How long those three weeks must have seemed to her!

I walked in the yard for a while before returning to the hut. I felt sad again. Had I, in losing my childhood, lost my carefree spirits too? Rejoining my companions, I shared my nuts with them. The taste, generally so refreshing when enjoyed with Canary wine, was now unrelieved bitterness.

Of course my father came often. He could visit me as freely as he liked. But we did not have much to say to each other.

Surrounded as we were by my companions, such visits could not be too intimate. Our talk wandered, and we would have been at a loss for words if my companions had not helped out.

During the fourth week we were allowed more liberty. Our wounds were either healed or making such good progress that there was no danger of relapse. By the end of that week we had completely recovered. The young men took the framework out of our hats and ripped open the seams of our *bou-bous*. Now we were wearing wide trousers, and we were very anxious to be seen again in public. We went for a walk in the town, very proud of ourselves, immensely proud of our new clothes, and talking at the tops of our voices, as if we were not already attracting enough attention.

We still remained in a group, and it was as a group that we made a round of visits to our concessions. We were fêted everywhere, and we always did justice to the banquets that awaited us. Now that we were almost well again—several of us were quite well; I had recovered completely—we had wonderful appetites.

Whenever an uncircumcised boy came too close to our happy band, we would seize him and belabor him playfully with our pompoms. But we were still forbidden all contact with girls, a ban which no one thought of breaking. We had been given strong warning that if any woman looked at us familiarly we ran the risk of being forever sterile. I caught sight of Fanta, who waved to me at a discreet distance. I answered by simply fluttering my eyelids. Was I still in love with her? I did not know. We had been so isolated from the world and had become so changed, even though a mere month had passed since we emerged from childhood into manhood. We had become so indifferent to all we had been before that I no longer knew quite where I was.

"Time," I thought, "time will help me to settle down again." But how? I had no idea.

Finally the day came when the healer decided we were completely recovered and ready to return to our parents. This did not involve an absolute change in our lives, though it almost did so for me. I was still at school, and I could no longer join in the excursions which my companions were making to the neighboring towns and villages. Nor could I participate in their labors in our healer's fields, work which they undertook to repay his care of us. My parents made an arrangement with him that exempted me.

When I did return to my concession, the whole family was waiting for me. My parents held me tight in their arms, especially my mother. It was as if she secretly wanted to proclaim that I was still her son and that my second birth had done nothing to alter that fact. My father watched us for a moment. Then he said to me, almost regretfully:

"From now on, this is your hut, my son."

The hut stood opposite my mother's.

"Yes," said my mother. "You will sleep there now. But, as you can see, I am still within earshot."

I opened the door of the hut. My clothes were laid out on the bed. I went up to it and took them in my hands one by one, then put them carefully back. They were men's clothes. Yes, the hut was opposite my mother's, I was still within earshot of her voice, but the clothes on the bed were men's clothes. I was a man!

"Are you pleased with them?" asked my mother.

Pleased? Naturally I was pleased. At least I think I was. They were fine clothes, they were. . . . I turned toward my mother. She was smiling at me sadly.

NINE

I was fifteen when I left home for Conakry where I was sent for a course of technical study at the École Georges Poiret, now known as the Technical College.

I was leaving my parents for the second time. The first had been immediately after I had passed my scholarship examination when I had acted as interpreter for an officer who had come to map the land in our district and in part of the neighboring Sudan. But on this second occasion I was to be away for a much longer time.

For a whole week my mother had been collecting provisions for me. Conakry is about four hundred miles from Kourous-

sa, and to my mother it was an unknown if not an unexplored
land where God alone knew if I would get enough to eat.
So she gathered *couscous,* meat, fish, yams, rice, and po-
tatoes. The week before, she had gone to the most celebrated
marabouts to consult them about my future and make sacrifices. She had offered up an ox in memory of her father
and had invoked the spirits of her ancestors that good fortune might attend me on a venture which in her eyes was
rather like going to live among savages. The fact that Conakry is the capital of Guinea only served to accentuate its
strangeness.

On the eve of my departure all the marabouts and witch-
doctors, friends and notables, and indeed anyone else who
cared to cross our threshold attended a magnificent feast in
our concession. For my mother believed that on this occasion
no one should be turned away. Representatives of all classes
of society must be present so that the blessing I was to take
with me might be complete. Moreover, this was the reason
the marabouts had requested such great quantities of food.
And so each guest, after having eaten his fill, took me by the
hand and blessed me, saying:

"May good fortune favor you! May your studies prosper!
And may the Lord protect you!"

The marabouts used much lengthier phrases. They began
by reciting a few quotations from the Koran which they
adapted to the present occasion. Then they invoked the name
of Allah. After that they blessed me.

I passed a wretched night. I was very much depressed, a
little upset, and I woke up several times. I thought I heard
groans. I guessed immediately that it was my mother. I got

up and went to her hut. She was tossing on her bed and moaning quietly. Perhaps I should have gone to her and tried to console her, but I did not know how she would take it. Maybe she would not have liked to think that she had been found weeping and wailing. I withdrew with a heavy heart. Was this what life was going to be like? Were tears a part of everything we did?

She woke me at dawn and I got up at once. I saw that her face was strained, but she was determined to keep control of herself and I said nothing. I pretended that her apparent calm had really convinced me. My luggage was piled up in the hut. Carefully wrapped and in a prominent position was a large bottle.

"What's in the bottle?" I asked.

"Do not break it."

"I'll look after it."

"Take great care of it. And every morning before you begin to study take a little sip."

"Is it supposed to be good for the brain?"

"It is indeed. It's the best thing there is. It comes from Kankan!"

I had already drunk some of this liquid. My teacher had forced me to when I was taking my scholarship examination. It is a magic potion possessing many qualities and particularly good for developing the brain. It is a curious mixture. Our marabouts have small boards on which they write prayers taken from the Koran. When they have written down the texts they erase them with water. The washing water is carefully collected and, when honey has been added to it, the resulting mixture is the essence of the elixir. If it had been bought—and bought at a very high price—in Kan-kan, a strongly Mohammedan town and the holiest of our native places, it must be a particularly potent drink. The evening before my father had given me a he-goat's horn con-taining talismans. I was to wear it always as a protection against evil spirits.

"Run and say your goodbyes now," said my mother.

I had to go and say farewell to the elders of our concession and to those of the concessions nearby. I went with a heavy heart. I had known these men and women since I was a baby. I had always known them. I had watched them living in this place and I had watched them disappear from it too. My father's mother had disappeared. Would I ever again see these people to whom I was now saying farewell? Overcome by doubts, I felt suddenly as if I were taking leave of the past itself. And wasn't that just what I was doing? Wasn't I leav-ing a part of my life behind me?

When I returned to my mother and saw her standing in tears beside my luggage I too began to weep. I threw myself into her arms. I begged her not to go with me to the station, for I thought that if she did I should never be able to tear myself away from her arms. She nodded consent. We em-braced for the last time and I almost ran out of the hut. My sisters and brothers and the apprentices carried my luggage.

My father quickly caught up with me and took my hand as he had done when I was a little boy. I slowed down. I felt weak and cried as if my heart were broken.

"Father!"

"I am listening."

"Am I really going away?"

"What else can you do? You know that you must."

"Yes."

And I began to cry again.

"Come, little one! You're a big boy now, aren't you?"

But his very presence, his kindness—and even more the fact that he was holding my hand—destroyed the last vestige of courage. He understood.

"I shall not go any further," he said. "We shall say goodbye to each other here. It would not do if we burst into tears at the station in front of your friends. And I don't want to leave your mother alone just now. She is very much upset. I am too! So are we all. But we must be brave. You be brave, my son. My brothers will look after you. Work hard. Work as you worked here. We have made many sacrifices for you. They must not go for nothing. Do you hear me?"

"Yes."

He was silent a moment, then went on:

"You see, I had no father to look after me. At least not for a very long time. When I was twelve I became an orphan and had to make my own way in life. It wasn't easy. The uncles in whose care I was left treated me more like a slave than a nephew. Not that I was a burden to them for very long. They hired me out to the Syrians right away. I was simply a domestic drudge, and I had to hand over everything I earned to my uncles. But even so it did not lessen their cruelty and greed. I always had to keep my own counsel and work hard to make a name for myself. You. . . . But I have said enough. Make the most of your opportunity. And make me proud of you. I ask no more. Will you?"

"I will, Father."

"Good! . . . Well, be brave, son. Goodbye."

"Father!"

He held me close. He had never held me so close before. "Goodbye, little one, goodbye."

Suddenly he let me go and walked away very fast. Perhaps he did not want me to see his tears. I went on along the road to the station. My eldest sister, my brothers, Sidafa and the younger apprentices went with me carrying my luggage. As we walked along we were joined by friends. Among them was Fanta. It was rather as if I were on my way to school again. All my companions were there. There had never been so many before. In fact, *wasn't* I on my way to school?

"Fanta, we're on the way to school."

The only answer was a faint smile. I was indeed on the way to school, but I was already alone. . . . There had never been so many of us, but I had never felt so alone. Although it was probably hardest for me we all shared the pain of parting. We spoke little. Soon we were standing on the station platform waiting for the train, but we had hardly said one word to one another. Weren't we all feeling everything that might have been said?

Several praise-singers had come to celebrate my departure. As soon as I reached the station they beset me with their flatteries. "Already thou art as wise as the White Man," they sang. "Verily thou art as wise as the White Man. In Conakry thou shalt take thy place even among the most illustrious." Such excessive praises dampened my vanity instead of inflaming it. After all, what *did* I know? I was still very far from "wise." The friends who were with me were as wise as I. I wanted to ask the praise-singers to stop or at least to moderate their flattery. But that would have been contrary to custom, so I kept silent. Perhaps their flatteries were not entirely useless. They made me determined to take my work seriously. It was true that I had always done so. But now I felt myself obliged to achieve, some day, everything they were chanting if I weren't to look like a fool when I came back.

Their flatteries had an additional effect. They kept me from thinking of the sadness I felt. They had made me smile before they began to embarrass me. Even though my companions had felt how ridiculous they were, and naturally they had, they didn't let it show. Perhaps we are so accustomed to the hyperboles of our praise-singers that we no longer take very much notice of them. But what about Fanta? No, she must have taken all those flatteries for truth. Fanta. . . . She never thought of smiling. Her eyes were filled with tears. Dear Fanta! . . . In despair I looked at my sister. She must surely know how I felt. She always felt as I did. But I saw she was tending to my luggage. She had already told me several times to keep an eye on it, and when our eyes met she told me so again.

"Don't worry. I will."

"You remember how many cases there are?"

"Yes."

"Good. Don't lose any. Remember you are staying the first night at Mamou. The train stops there for the night."

"You don't have to explain everything to me. I'm not a child."

"No, but you don't know what sort of people they'll be down there. Keep your luggage beside you and count it from time to time. You understand? Keep your eye on it."

"Yes."

"And be careful with strangers."

"Yes."

But I had stopped listening to her and smiling at the chants of the praise-singers. My sadness had returned. My little brothers had slipped their hands into mine and I kept thinking how warm and soft they were. I kept thinking too that the train would soon be here and that I should have to release those small hands. I began to feel afraid the train would come. I began to hope it would be late. Sometimes it was. Perhaps it would be, today. I looked at the clock. It was late! . . . But suddenly it appeared.

In the uproar of departure it seemed to me that I had eyes for my brothers alone. They were pushed about in the crowd; they were bewildered; but they always managed to be in front of the rest. My eyes kept returning to them. Did I care for them that much? I don't know. Often I had paid no attention to them. When I left for school in the morning they had usually been asleep or were being bathed. When I returned in the afternoon I never had much time to spend with them. But now they were all I could see. Was it the warmth of their hands which I still felt and which made me remember that my father had taken me by the hand just now? Perhaps. Perhaps this was the last bit of warmth from the hut where I had been born.

My luggage was handed to me through the window and I put it all on the seats. My sister gave me some last words of advice as useless as all the others. Everyone had something nice to say to me, Fanta and Sidafa especially. But in all the waving of hands and scarves that accompanied the

departure of the train I really saw only my brothers who ran
the length of the platform, the length of the train, shouting
goodbye. Where the platform ended, my sister and Fanta
joined them. I looked at my brothers waving their caps, at
my sister and Fanta waving their handkerchiefs, and then
suddenly they disappeared from sight, long before the first
bend in the track, for a sudden mist enveloped them and
tears blinded me. . . . For a long time I lay in a corner of
my compartment with my luggage strewn all about me and
before me that final image: my little brothers, my sister,
Fanta. . . .

Toward midday the train reached Dabola. By this time
I had sorted out my luggage and counted it. My interest in
people and things was beginning to revive somewhat. I
heard *Peul* spoken. Dabola is on the borders of the *Peul*
country. The great plain where I had lived until now, that
plain so rich, so poor, so sunburnt—yet so familiar and
friendly—was giving way to the foothills of the Fouta-Djallon.

The train began its journey again toward Mamou. Soon
the lofty cliffs of the mountains appeared. They blocked the
horizon, and the train set out to conquer them. It was a
very slow conquest, almost a hopeless one. So slow and hopeless, that sometimes the train went at barely more than a
walking pace. This country, new to me, too new and too
rugged, disturbed rather than enchanted me. I did not notice
how beautiful it was.

I arrived at Mamou a little before nightfall. As the train
does not go on from there until the next day, the passengers
spend the night in a hotel or with friends. A former apprentice of my father's who had been told I was passing

through, had offered me his hospitality. He gave me a most cordial welcome. Actually—but perhaps he had forgotten the difference in climate—he lodged me in a dark hut on top of a hill where I had sufficient leisure—more than I wanted— to feel the chill night and the keen air of the Fouta-Djallon. Mountains certainly did not agree with me!

The next day I continued my journey. But a complete change had taken place. Was I getting acclimated already? I do not know. But my feelings about mountains had changed, so much so that from Mamou to Kindia I did not leave the window for a moment. I was enchanted with the succession of peaks and precipices, torrents and cascades of water, wooded slopes and deep valleys. Water gushed and flowed everywhere, animating everything. It was a wonderful spectacle. A little terrifying too, whenever the train seemed to go too close to the edge of a precipice. Because the air was extraordinarily pure, I could see everything in the minutest detail. It was a happy land; it seemed happy. There were innumerable flocks of sheep grazing, and the shepherds waved as we passed.

When we stopped at Kindia I no longer heard *Peul* being spoken. This time it was *Soussou*, the dialect of Conakry. I listened for a while but I understood little of what was being said.

Now we were descending toward the coast and Conakry. The train went on and on. Just as it had seemed to puff painfully up the mountains, now it rolled joyfully down. But the landscape was no longer what it had been between Mamou and Kindia. It was no longer so picturesque. There was less movement in it; it was less wild, more domesticated.

Vast stretches of banana and palm trees, symmetrically laid out, followed each other. The heat was overpowering and increased as we approached the coast. The air was heavy, humid.

The brightly lit peninsula of Conakry appeared with evening. I saw it from afar, a huge shining flower floating on the sea, its stalk held to the mainland. The water shone softly, shone like the sky, but unlike the sky in its quivering animation. Almost immediately the flower began to expand and the water to recede. For a few moments more it extended on both sides of the stalk. Then it disappeared. We were rapidly approaching Conakry. When we arrived among the lights of the peninsula—the very heart of the flower—the train halted.

A tall, imposing man came up to me. I had never seen him before—or rather I had seen him too many years ago to remember—but from the way he looked at me I guessed he was my father's brother.

"Are you my Uncle Mamadou?" I asked.

"Yes. And you are my nephew Laye. I knew you at once. The living image of your mother. Really, I could not have missed you. How are your mother and father? . . . But come along. We'll have time to discuss that later. Now you must have something to eat and a good night's rest. Come on; you'll find dinner ready, and your room is in order."

That was the first night I had passed in a European-style house. Was it the unfamiliarity, or the humid heat of the town, or the fatigue of two days in the train that kept me from sleeping? Yet it was a very comfortable house: the room I slept in was large, and the bed soft, softer than any I had previously slept on. Also I had been welcomed as warmly as if I had been a son of the house. In spite of this, I missed Kouroussa. I missed my little hut. All my thoughts centered on Kouroussa. Once again I saw my mother and my father, my brothers and my sisters, my friends. I was in Conakry and yet I wasn't. I was really at Kouroussa. But, no—I was in both places. I was ambivalent. And I felt very lonely, despite the affectionate welcome.

"Well," said my uncle when I came down in the morning, "have you slept well?"

"Yes."

"No, you haven't. The change has been too abrupt. But you will soon get used to it here. You'll sleep better tonight. Don't you think so?"

"Yes."

"And what are you planning for today?"

"I don't know. Should I visit the school?"

"We'll do that tomorrow together. Have a look around town today. This is the last day of your holidays, after all."

I walked into town. It was very different from Kouroussa. The avenues were as straight as rulers and crossed each other at right angles. They were lined with mango trees which were also planted elsewhere in shady groups. Their thick shade was always welcome, for the heat was overpowering. Not that it was much worse than at Kouroussa—perhaps it was even less intense—but the humidity was greater. The houses were all embowered in flowers and foliage. Many looked submerged in all the greenery, drowned in a frantic proliferation. And then I saw the sea. . . .

Suddenly at the end of an avenue, I saw it. I stood a long time observing its vastness, watching the waves roll in, one

after another, to break against the red rocks of the shore. In
the distance, despite the mist around them, I saw some very
green islands. It was the most astonishing spectacle that had
ever confronted me. At night, from the train, I had only
glimpsed the sea. I had formed no real idea of its size, nor
even less of its movement, of the kind of fascination one feels
toward its endless movement. Now that the whole spectacle
lay before me I could scarcely come away.

"How did you like the town?" asked my uncle when I
returned.

"Wonderful."

"Yes. But a bit hot, to judge from your clothes. You're
perspiring. Go and change. You'll have to do that several
times a day here. But be quick about it. Dinner is almost
ready and your aunts want to serve it."

My uncle lived with his two wives, my aunts Awa and
N'Gady, and a younger brother, my Uncle Sékou. Like my
uncles, each of my aunts had her own room which she occupied with her own children.

From the beginning my aunts were fond of me, so much so
that soon they treated me like one of their own children.
The children, much younger than I, were not told I was
their cousin. They thought I was their elder brother and
treated me as such. No day passed without their climbing on
my knees. Later, when I spent all my holidays at my uncle's
house, they would run to meet me. As soon as they heard or
saw me, they came racing. If they were absorbed in a game,
my aunts would scold them: "What's this?" they would cry.
"It's a whole week since you've seen your big brother and
you haven't greeted him." Yes, my aunts really put themselves

out to take my mother's place. They did so all the time I was with them. Their indulgence was so great that they never scolded me when I misbehaved—which rather confused me. They were high-principled and had the most lively dispositions. It did not take me long to find out that, between them, they comprehended more than most people do. I lived actually amidst a deeply united family where all domestic quarreling was strictly forbidden. I think that the placid and almost invisible authority of my uncle was the foundation for this sense of peace and unity.

My Uncle Mamadou was a little younger than my father. He was tall and strong, always very correctly dressed, calm and dignified. He was a man who made himself felt at once. Like my father he had been born in Kouroussa but had left it when he was very young. He had gone to school there, and then had come to Conakry to continue his studies at the École Normale de Goré. I believe he worked as a teacher for a short time, but went into business soon afterward. When I came to Conakry he was the chief accountant in a French establishment. I gradually became better acquainted with him, and the more I knew him the more I loved and respected him.

He was a Mohammedan—as we all are, I may add—but more orthodox than most of us. His observance of the Koran was scrupulously correct. He neither smoked nor drank and was absolutely honest. He wore European clothes only for work. As soon as he came home he undressed and put on a *boubou* which had to be immaculate, and said his prayers. On leaving the École Normale he had taken up the study of Arabic. He had learned it thoroughly by himself, using bilingual books and a dictionary. Now he could speak that language as well as French, though he never did so to create an impression. It was simply his desire for a deeper knowledge of religion that had persuaded him to learn the language of the Prophet. The Koran guided him in everything. I never saw him in a temper, nor quarreling with his wives. He was always greatly esteemed in Conakry, and I merely had to mention my relationship to him to share some of his prestige. I regarded him as a saintly personage.

My Uncle Sékou, the youngest of my father's brothers, was not distinguished by this same immaculate conduct. In one way—his youth—he was much closer to me. His exuberance delighted me; it manifested itself in a great flow of words. When he spoke he became inexhaustible. I loved to listen to him—everyone loved to—because he spoke so eloquently and said such interesting things. I will add that there was a serious side to his exuberance and that this seriousness was essentially the same as my Uncle Mamadou's. When I knew him he was still unmarried—only engaged—another reason why I was closer to him than to his brother. I never found fault with him. He was more an elder brother to me than an uncle. He worked for the Conakry-Niger railway.

When the holidays were over my Uncle Mamadou took me to my new school.

"Work hard," he said, "and the Lord will look out for you. You can tell me your first impressions on Sunday."

In the courtyard, where I was given my first instructions, and in the dormitory where I went to put away my clothes, I found other students who had come from Upper Guinea. We became friendly and I felt less lonely. A little later we entered our classroom. All of us, new and old students alike, assembled in the same vast room. I was attentive to everything, since I hoped to profit from some of the lessons given the older students while paying attention to whatever went on in my own class. But almost at once I saw that no great distinction was made between older and younger students. Instead, the teachers seemed prepared to repeat to the older students the lessons they had already crammed into them two or three times since the first year. "We'll see," I said to myself. But, all the same, I was disturbed. I thought such a method of teaching did not augur well.

To start us off, a very simple text was dictated. When the teacher marked the copies I could not understand how they contained so many errors. None of my friends in Kouroussa would have had any trouble with it. Afterwards we were given a problem to solve. Two of us got the right answer. I was stunned. Was this the school where I was to enjoy the advantages of higher education? I felt as if I were going back several years to the beginners' class in Kouroussa. And that is exactly how it was. The whole week passed without my having learned a thing. On Sunday I complained loudly to my uncle.

"I've learned nothing. I already know everything they've taught us. Is it really worth while going to that school? I might as well go back to Kouroussa at once!"

"No," advised my uncle. "Wait a while."

"There's nothing to wait for. I could see that immediately."

"Don't be so impatient. Are you always this way? Perhaps the school does operate on a low level so far as general subjects go, but it can give you practical training which you won't find anywhere else. Have you been in the workshops?"

I showed him my hands. They were covered with scratches and the tips of my fingers were scarred.

"But I don't want to be a laborer."

"Why not?"

"I don't want to be despised."

So far as general opinion went there was a tremendous difference between the students at our school and those at Camille Guy. We were looked upon simply as future laborers. It was certain that we would not become skilled workmen. At the most we might become foremen. Unlike the students at Camille Guy, we could never enter the colleges in Dakar.

"Listen to me carefully," said my uncle. "All the students who come from Kouroussa are scornful of the Technical School. They all dream of becoming clerks. Do you aspire to that sort of career? Clerks are thirteen to the dozen. If you really want to be a clerk, change your school. But remember this: if I were twenty years younger and had to go to school again I would not go to the École Normale. No! I would learn a good trade in a technical school. A good trade would have taken me a lot further."

"But I might as well never have left my father's forge."

"You needn't have. But, tell me, have you never had ambitions beyond the forge?"

Now I had ambitions. But I would never realize them by becoming a manual laborer. I had no more respect for manual laborers than most people have.

"But who said anything about manual labor? A technician is not necessarily a manual laborer. And, anyhow, there's more he can do. He's a man who directs others and knows how things should be done. He can turn his hand to anything should the need arise. Men who are in charge of businesses aren't always this versatile, and that will be to your advantage. Believe me, stay where you are. And I'm going to tell you something you don't know: your school is about to be reorganized. There will be great changes soon, and instruction in general subjects will equal that of Camille Guy."

Was I finally convinced by my uncle's arguments? Perhaps not altogether. But my Uncle Sékou, and even my aunts, argued as he did, so I stayed at the Technical School.

For four days out of six I was in the workshops filing bits of iron or planing boards under the direction of a monitor. It seemed to be easy and interesting. But it was not so easy as it looked at first sight. First of all I had had no practice, and in the second place the long hours of standing at a bench were a strain. I don't know how it happened—was it being too much on my feet or an infection from a splinter of metal or wool?—but my feet began to swell and I developed an ulcer. I believe that at Kouroussa such a growth would not have been malignant. It would not even have happened. But here in this burning, moisture-laden heat, in this climate to which my body had not had time to become adapted, the ulcer rapidly grew worse. I was hospitalized.

My spirits drooped. The more than Spartan fare which was given us in this otherwise magnificent hospital was not really intended to raise the spirits. But as soon as my aunts learned what had happened they brought my meals each day. My uncles visited me too and kept me company. Without them I should have been really miserable, lonely, in that city whose ways were foreign to me, whose climate was hostile, and whose dialect I could barely follow. All around me only *Soussou* was spoken. And I am a Malinké. Except for French the only language I speak is *Malinké*.

Then I began to think it was silly to lie there twiddling my thumbs, breathing sticky air, and sweating night and day. I began to think it was even sillier not to be at school instead of sweltering in such a suffocating atmosphere and in such useless immobility. What was I doing but wasting my time in a most unfortunate fashion? The ulcer wasn't getting any better. It wasn't getting any worse either. It just stayed the same. . . .

The school year passed slowly, very slowly. It seemed endless to me, as endless as the interminable rains that beat down for days and sometimes for weeks on the corrugated iron roofs. As endless as my interminable sickness. Then, by a strange coincidence which I can not explain, I got well just as the school year ended. It was high time. I was choking, bubbling over with impatience. . . . I set off for Kouroussa as if for the promised land.

When I returned to Conakry in October after the vacation,
the change my uncle had spoken of was in full swing. The
school had been entirely reorganized. New classrooms had
been built, a new director had been appointed, and teachers
had come from France. The instruction in technical subjects
was excellent, and that in general subjects very good. I no
longer envied the students at Camille Guy. I was getting the
same kind of education as they, and technical and practical
training besides. The older students had left. They had all
been hired by the Conakry-Niger Railway. So everything began anew for us first-year students. My Uncle Mamadou had

not deceived me. I worked very hard at my studies and each term my name was on the honor roll. My uncle was overjoyed.

That was the year I made friends with Marie.

Whenever I think about our friendship, and I often do— I am forever dreaming of it—it seems to me that in all those years it was the best thing that happened to me. Nothing in those years of exile meant more. It was not that I needed affection. My aunts and uncles gave me all they could. But I was at that age when the heart can not rest until it has found some object to cherish, when it can endure no restraint but its own, more powerful and more demanding than all others. Are we not always so? Are we not always consumed with longing? Do our hearts ever rest?

Marie was a student at the girls' high school. Before her father studied medicine and went into practice in Bela, he had been a school friend of my Uncle Mamadou's, and they were still very intimate. So Marie used to spend all her Sundays at my uncle's. Like me, she found another home there. She was a half-caste. Her skin was very light, almost white. She was very beautiful, surely the most beautiful girl in her school. I thought her as beautiful as a fairy. She was sweet and charming and had a wonderfully even temper. She had exceptionally long hair which hung down to her waist.

On Sundays she arrived at my uncle's early, usually much earlier than I, for I used to loiter in the streets. As soon as she came she went from room to room saying hello to everyone. Then she went to my Aunt Awa's apartment. She would put down her satchel, take off her European clothes, put on the Guinea tunic which allowed her greater freedom of movement, and help my aunt with the housework. My aunts liked her very much and were as good to her as to their own children, but they often teased me about her.

"Well, Marie," they would say, "what have you done with your husband?"

"I don't have one yet."

"Really? I thought our nephew was your husband."

"I'm not old enough."

"Well, when will you be?"

But Marie only smiled and said nothing.

"A smile is not an answer," my aunt Awa would say. "Can't you give us a straightforward answer?"

"I can't, Aunt Awa."

"That's just what I'm complaining about! When I was your age I didn't have so many secrets."

"Do I have so many? Tell about the time when you were a girl. You must have had the whole canton running after you, you're so pretty."

"Ever see such a sly puss? I start the talk about her and she turns it around to me! And not content with that, it's my so-called successes she drags out. Are all the girls in high school so clever?"

My aunts had been aware of our friendship from the start and they approved of it. Not only that, they encouraged it. They loved us both and they would have liked us to become engaged despite our youth. But that was asking more than our shyness would allow.

When I came home from school I too used to make a tour of the house, stopping for a moment in each room to exchange a few words, and often remaining a long time with my

Uncle Mamadou. He loved to hear every detail of what I
had learned, and to criticize what I had done. When I went
into Aunt Awa's apartment she invariably greeted me by
saying:

"Look, you've kept Madame Camara Number Three waiting again!"

Madame Camara Number Three was the name she gave
Marie. Aunt Awa was Madame Camara Number One and
Aunt N'Gady was Number Two. I used to take the joke with
good grace and bow to Marie: "Good day, Madame Camara
Number Three."

"Good day, Laye."

And we would shake hands. But Aunt Awa thought us very
undemonstrative. She sighed: "What slow-pokes you are!
Goodness, I've never seen such slow-pokes."

I would steal away without replying. I did not have Marie's
gift of repartee, and Aunt Awa might soon have defeated me
with her banter. I continued on my way, my little cousins
at my heels, or hanging on to my clothes. I carried the smallest ones in my arms or perched on my shoulders. Finally I
sat down wherever I felt like it, usually in the garden for the
children were particularly noisy by then. I played with them
while waiting for dinner.

Because I had a naturally good appetite and hadn't eaten
anything since I awoke, I always arrived famished. On a half
holiday it would have been a sin to touch the mess we were
served at school. I never did, considering it sufficient punishment to have to eat it the other six days of the week. My
aunts, who had always cooked something very special, would
have liked me to take my meals with Marie. But how could

I? No, I could not allow it, and I don't think Marie would have liked it either. We would have felt shy about eating at the same table. We were so very shy, in a way which was incomprehensible and almost offensive to my aunts. Marie and I never even discussed the possibility, we were so conventional. We never thought of meeting again until the meal was over.

Then we nearly always went to my Uncle Sékou's apartment. His was the quietest section of the house. Not that he was a quiet man—as I have remarked, he was a prodigious orator—but since he was unmarried he was often out and we were left alone.

He used to leave his phonograph and records for us, and Marie and I would dance. Of course we danced very circumspectly. In Guinea it is not customary for couples to dance in each other's arms. We danced facing each other, but without touching. At the very most we held hands, though this was not usual. Need I say that in our shyness we desired nothing better? Would we have danced together otherwise? I hardly know. I think not, though like all Africans, dancing was in our blood.

But we did more than dance. Marie would take her exercise books out of her satchel and ask me to help her. It was the best opportunity I had to display my talents. I always explained everything, never missing a single detail.

"You see, first of all you find the quotient of. . . . Marie! Are you listening?"

"Yes."

"Well, be sure to remember that first you must find out. . . ."

But Marie did not pay much attention. Perhaps she didn't pay any. What she wanted was to see the answer written at the bottom of a problem she could never have solved without my help. The rest did not interest her. The details, the reasons, the methods, the pedantic tone of voice which I probably used—all these were lost on her. She sat staring into space. What could she be dreaming about? I did not know then. When I think about it now, I wonder if she dreamt about us. Perhaps not. But I see that some explanation is needed here.

Marie loved me and I loved her, but we never called what we felt by the sweet and terrible name of "love." Perhaps it was not exactly love, though there was something of that in it. What was it? It was something big and noble, a marvelous tenderness and an immense happiness. I mean happiness unalloyed, pure, and as yet untroubled by desire. Perhaps it was more happiness than love, though the one can not exist without the other. I could not take Marie by the hand without trembling. I could not feel the light touch of her hair without being deeply moved. Happiness and passion! Maybe that is what love really is. But it was a child-like passion, and we were still children. Officially I was a man. I had been initiated. Was that enough to make me one? Years alone make a man, and I was not old enough. . . .

Did Marie take a different view of our friendship? I don't think so. Was she more worldly-wise than I? Girls often are, but I don't think she was. Her modesty—our common modesty—makes me think not. Yet passion was most important in the lives of the people around her, and she must have been aware of it. Was she? I don't know. I don't know whether her attitude was conscious or purely instinctive. But I remember that she seemed quite blind to it.

For I was not the only one in love with her, though I was perhaps the only one who loved her so innocently. All my friends were in love with her. When we were tired of listening to records and dancing, and when we had finished our lessons, we used to go out. I would put her on my bicycle and the young men of Conakry, especially my school friends and the students from Camille Guy, watched us enviously as we rode by. They all wanted to go out walking with Marie, but she used to ignore them. She had eyes only for me.

I am not boasting when I set this down, though at the time I was proud enough of my luck. No. It is poignantly sweet to remember. It fills my dreams with inexpressible melancholy.

Usually we rode in the direction of the shore. Once there, we would sit and look at the sea. I loved to watch it. When I suddenly came upon it while first exploring Conakry, I had fallen in love with it at once. That vast plain. . . . Yes, perhaps that vast plain of water reminded me of another plain: Upper Guinea where I had grown up. . . . But, had I found it less attractive after that first glimpse I still would have come to watch it, for Marie liked nothing better. She would sit and watch until she could watch no more.

Seen from the shore, the sea is very beautiful—streaked with brilliant colors. It is opaque at the edges, mingling the blue of the sky with the shining green of the coco and palm trees on shore, and fringed with foam—a rainbow fringe. Further out, it has a pearly lustre. The islands of coco trees, which float in the distance, in a slightly misted, vaporous radiance, have such fresh, delicate shades that one is enchanted by the sight. A slight breeze from the open sea tempers the heat of the town.

"One can breathe!" I would exclaim. "One can breathe here!"

"Yes."

"See those little islands out there? I'll bet one can breathe even better there."

"I'm sure of it."

"Wouldn't you like to go there?"

"But there's water on all sides."

"Of course."

"Who would visit them? They're desert islands."

"Fishermen go. With a boat we'd be there in half an hour."

"A boat?"

Out of the corner of her eye she seemed to measure the violence of the waves as they dashed against the red rocks.

"I don't want to go in a boat. Can't you see how rough it is?"

The sea *was* rough. It thundered violently against the shore. A boat seemed a very fragile thing to venture out in. The fishermen were not afraid, but we weren't fishermen. We needed to know, as they did, where the sea was wild, and how to tame its wildness. I knew nothing at all about the sea. I used to go out on the Niger, but the Niger flowed tranquilly; in times of flood it was a little rough. The sea was never tranquil; there was no end to its restless movement.

"We might ask some of the fishermen to take us out," I would suggest.

"Why? You don't need them. You don't even need a boat. Your two eyes will do. If you watch the islands for a long time, and stare at them without blinking, or look at one of them so long that it begins to tremble, it's almost as though you'd landed on it. You *are* on the island."

"Are you?"

"Listen. . . . You can even hear the breeze rustling in the coco trees."

The sound was really over our heads in the rustling fronds of the coco trees along the shore. Our illusion faded. We laughed.

What else did we talk about? School, of course. We exchanged the latest gossip. Perhaps we spoke of the past, or of Kouroussa, and my holidays at Tindican. What else? I really don't know. Our hearts were hidden from each other. They were like the green islands that trembled on the horizon. We traveled there in thought, but could not approach them in words. Our friendship must remain unspoken. A single word would have changed it irrevocably, and we did not expect it to change. We were always everything to each other.

It was already dusk when we started home. "Is the day gone?" I wondered as I pedaled along. Yes, this Sunday was almost over. During the week, time seemed immobile. Sundays it raced along uninterruptedly. It disappeared as rapidly on rainy Sundays when we remained in the house. The dreaded sheets of rain, so interminable when they fell outside the schoolroom, cleared away when I was with Marie. . . .

The years went by in this fashion. I was a long way from

my parents and Kouroussa, and the great plain where I had been born. I often thought of them all. Yet I spent every Sunday in a family where everyone loved me.

At the end of the third year I took the examinations for a certificate of proficiency. We were told that a minimum of sixty per cent was required to pass the tests in technical and classical subjects and that the Conakry engineers were to be our examiners. Then the school designated the fourteen most likely candidates. Fortunately my name was among them.

I was determined to pass. I had worked hard for three years. I had never forgotten my promise to my father, nor the one I had made to myself. I had always been among the three highest students and hoped to maintain my rating. But I wrote my mother to see the marabouts and get their help. Was I especially superstitious at that time? I do not think so. I simply believed that nothing could be obtained without God's help, and that, even if His will were predetermined, our actions, though these too were predetermined, influenced it. And I felt that the marabouts were my natural intermediaries.

My aunts offered up sacrifices and presented *cola* nuts to the various persons the marabouts indicated they had consulted. I could see they were very anxious about me. I believe they were as anxious as my mother. Marie was even more so, if possible. She didn't set much store by her own studies, but she would have been deeply distressed not to see my name in the list of successful candidates in the official newspaper of French Guinea. My aunts told me that she also had been to the marabouts, and I really think that touched me more than anything else.

Finally the examination came. It lasted three days. Three days of agony. But the marabouts must have given me all the help they could. Of the seven candidates who passed I was first.

ELEVEN

Each time I went home for my vacation I found my hut newly plastered with white clay. My mother could hardly wait to show me the improvements she had made from year to year.

Originally it had been like the other huts, but gradually it began to acquire a European look. I say "began to," for the resemblance was never exact. Yet I was keenly aware of the changes, not only because they made the hut more comfortable, but even more because they were tangible proof of how much my mother loved me. Though I spent most of the year in Conakry, I was still her favorite. That was easy to see, and the appearance of my hut emphasized the fact.

"What do you think of it?" she would ask.

"It's wonderful."

And I would give her a great hug, which was all the thanks she expected. It was indeed wonderful. I didn't suspect how much ingenuity had been used, how much trouble she had taken to create—out of the simplest materials—her modest imitations of European comforts.

The main article of furniture, and the one which immediately caught the eye, was the divan-bed. Originally it had been just like the one in her own hut, like any other in Upper Guinea. It was made of clay bricks. First she had removed the bricks from the center, leaving only two supports, one at the foot and one at the head; instead of the bricks she had substituted planks. Then she had put a mattress stuffed with rice straw on the improvised bedstead. It made a crude but comfortable bed, and one that was fairly spacious, big enough for three or even four people.

But it was hardly spacious enough to accommodate all the innumerable friends, girls as well as boys, who visited me in the evenings. It was the only place where they could sit. They piled up on it, as each one made a comfortable place for himself. Late comers had to sit on the edge. I can not remember just how—heaped together as we were—we managed to find room to strum our guitars and breathe enough air for singing.

I don't think my mother liked these gatherings. She put up with them, probably comforting herself with the thought that at least I was in my own concession and not hanging around God knew where. My father thought they were quite proper. Since I scarcely saw him at all during the day—occupied as I was in visiting one friend or another or going off somewhere on some more extensive trip—he would come at night and knock on my door. I would cry: "Come in!" When he would enter he would say good evening to everyone and ask me how I had spent the day. After a few more words he would go away. He knew that he was welcome—he really was —but that he was a damper on gatherings as youthful and lively as ours.

My mother's attitude was completely different. Her hut was close to mine and the doors of the hut faced each other. She had only to take a step to be inside mine. She would do so without warning, never knocking at the door. Suddenly there she would be, and she would study everyone carefully before saying good evening.

She was not so interested in my men friends. They were my own affair and didn't matter. No, it was only the girls she inspected, and she was quick to note those she didn't like. I have to admit that I sometimes entertained young women of rather loose habits and slightly tarnished reputations. But how could I forbid them to come? Did I even want to? They might be a little more worldly wise than was necessary, but they were generally the most amusing. My mother thought otherwise and she always came straight to the point.

"What are you doing here? Go home. If I see you here again I'll tell your mother. I've warned you!"

If the girl did not leave fast enough, my mother would pull her from the divan and push her toward the door: "Go home with you!"

And she would wave her hands as if she were driving away some overadventurous fowl. Only then would she say good evening to the others.

I did not care for her behavior. Reports of these insults spread through the district. Whenever I invited a girl to visit me she would very likely ask: "What if your mother catches me?"

"She won't eat you."

"No, but she'll show me the door."

I would stand before her, wondering: "Has my mother really any reason to disapprove of her?" I did not always know. Since I lived in Conakry most of the year I wasn't versed in all the gossip of Kouroussa. But I could scarcely ask her: "Have you been talked about? Have you had any affairs my mother knows about?" I was exasperated.

As I grew older I became more passionate. I no longer had diffident friendships and sly love affairs. There were other girls besides Marie and Fanta—although at first they had been the only ones. But Marie was vacationing at Bela with her father and Fanta was my "steady." I kept a proper distance. Even if I had wished to go further—and I did not—custom forbade it. The other girls were unimportant, but they did exist. Couldn't my mother understand?

She understood only too well. She often got up in the middle of the night to make sure that I was in bed alone. Usually she made her inspection around midnight and she would strike a match to light up my bed. If I were still awake I would feign sleep. Then, as if disturbed by the lighted match, I would "wake" with a start.

"What is it?"

"Are you asleep?"

"I *was* asleep. Why do you wake me?"

"Go back to sleep."

"How can I sleep if you're always waking me?"

"Don't be upset. Go to sleep."

But this kind of treatment annoyed me. I complained of it to Kouyaté and Check Omar who were my best friends at the time.

"I'm old enough to take care of myself. I live in my own hut. But how can I call it my own if people can intrude every hour of the day and night?"

"It shows how much your mother loves you. Is that what you're complaining about?"

Yet I couldn't help thinking that her affection for me might have been a little less jealous and tyrannical. It was obvious that Check and Kouyaté had more freedom than I.

"Don't brood over it so," Kouyaté advised. "Play your guitar for us."

I would take down my guitar which Kouyaté had taught me to play. In the evening, instead of staying in my hut, we would stroll through the town strumming our guitars while Check played the banjo; all three of us would sing in harmony. Often girls who had already retired would wake and listen as we passed their concessions. If they were friends and recognized our voices they rose and dressed hastily and ran to join us. Soon there would be not three or four of us but six, ten, sometimes even fifteen making the sleeping streets reverberate.

Kouyaté and Check had attended primary school with me. They were both clever, extremely good at mathematics. I can still remember that they would jump up with the correct answer almost before the teacher had finished dictating the problem. Their suprising speed had amazed me and discouraged me, although I of course had had my triumphs when it came to French. But from school on—despite or because of our competitive spirit—we had been friends, though it had been a schoolboys' friendship, the sort that usually doesn't last.

Our real friendship had not begun until after I had left to go to school at Conakry and Kouyaté and Check were attending high school at Popodra and Dakar respectively. We wrote one another many long letters describing our school life and when holidays came we all met once more in Kouroussa. Soon we were inseparable.

At first our parents were not too happy about our friendship. We would disappear for whole days, forgetting about our meals. Sometimes all three of us would turn up in the same concession so that at dinner there would be unexpected guests. Such behavior was undoubtedly a little free, but our parents did not frown on our friendship very long. They realized soon that they would have extra guests only every third day and they accepted this just and equitable system of rotation.

"But you might have let me know!" my mother would complain. "I would have cooked something special."

"No. We didn't want anything special, only the usual daily meal."

The holidays ending Kouyaté and Check's third year in school—it was my second year (I had lost a year in the hospital)—I saw my friends again. They had received teaching certificates and were waiting for positions. I had expected as much, but still I was pleased at their success and congratulated them heartily. When I asked them how they felt, Check said he was exhausted.

"I worked very hard, and I haven't quite recovered."

Was it merely that he was tired? He looked ill and his face was drawn. A few days later when I was alone with Kouyaté I asked him if he thought it was simply overwork.

"No," he said. "Check is sick. He hasn't any appetite and he is losing weight. Besides, his stomach is swelling."

"Shouldn't we say something to him?"

"Oh, I think he knows."

"Isn't he doing anything about it?"

"I don't think he is. He's in no pain and apparently he thinks he'll recover gradually."

"But if he doesn't?"

We had no idea what to do. We did not want to frighten Check and yet we felt that something had to be done.

"I'll speak to my mother," I said.

But when I did she interrupted me: "Check Omar is seriously ill. I've been watching him for several days. I must bring it to his mother's attention."

Check's mother did what was always done in the circumstances: she consulted the medicine men. They prescribed massages and herb tea. But these remedies had no effect. His stomach continued to swell and his face became gray. Still he was not alarmed.

"I'm not in any pain," he said. "I haven't much appetite, but whatever it is, it will probably go as quickly as it came."

I don't know whether Check had any great confidence in the medicine men. Probably not. By now we had spent too many years in school to have real faith. Yet our medicine men are not mere charlatans. Many of them have great knowledge and can effect real cures. Check was aware of this. But he must have realized that in this instance their remedies were not effective, and that was why he said, "It will probably go as quickly as it came," putting his faith in the passage of time. For a few days his words heartened us, but then he began to suffer terribly. He had violent pains which would make him cry out in agony.

"Look," Kouyaté told him, "the medicine men haven't done you any good. Let's go to the dispensary."

We went. The doctor examined Check and sent him to the hospital. He did not say what was wrong with him, but now we knew that it was a serious illness and Check also knew this. Would the white doctor succeed where our own medicine men had failed? Good does not always overcome evil, and we were deeply troubled. We took turns watching at the bedside where our poor friend writhed in agony. His stomach was swollen and hard and cold—as if this part of him were already dead. Whenever the attacks became more severe we ran distractedly for the doctor. "Doctor, come quick!" But medicine was of no avail.

We stayed at his bedside a week along with his mother, his brothers, my mother and Kouyaté's. Toward the end of the week suddenly the pain ceased and we bade the others go and rest. He was sleeping peacefully and we did not dare wake him. We watched him sleep and were hopeful. His face had grown so thin that bones were visible through the skin, but his features were no longer drawn and his lips seemed to smile. Then gradually the pain returned, the lips ceased smiling, and Check awoke. He began to tell us his last wishes.

He told us how we should distribute his books and to whom
we should give his banjo. His voice became fainter and fainter
and we could not always catch the end of a sentence. Then
he said goodbye to us once more. When he ceased speaking
it was nearly midnight. Then, as the dispensary clock finished
the twelve strokes, he died. . . .

I feel as if I were living through those days and nights
again. I have never spent any that were more wretched.
Kouyaté and I wandered about as if we had gone out of our
minds; our thoughts were full of Check. To have lived so
many happy days . . . and then for everything to be over!
"Check . . . ," I kept saying to myself. We both kept saying
it to ourselves. We had to restrain ourselves from saying his
name out loud. But his ghost kept us company. We would
see him in the center of his concession, laid out on his bier;
he would be under his winding sheet, ready to be laid in the
earth. We would see him in the earth itself, lying at the bottom of his grave, his head raised a bit, waiting for the covering
of planks to be put down on him, waiting for the leaves, the
great mounds of leaves, for the heavy earth itself.

"Check! . . . Check! . . ." But I could not say his name;
we are not allowed to address the dead aloud. And yet at night
it was almost as if I did. Suddenly he would be standing before me. I would wake up bathed in sweat. I was afraid, and
so was Kouyaté. For though we loved Check's ghost we feared
it almost as much as we loved it, and we no longer dared
sleep alone; we no longer dared face our dreams alone. . . .

Now whenever I think of those far off days I can not say
exactly what it was I was so frightened of. Probably that is
because I no longer look upon death as I did then. It has

become simpler than it was. I think of those days and think only that Check has gone before us along God's highway, and that all of us will one day walk along that highway which is no more frightening than the others, indeed far less frightening. The others? . . . Yes, the others, the highways of life, the ones we set foot on when we are born and which are only the temporary highways of exile. . . .

TWELVE

When I returned to Kouroussa with my proficiency certificate in my pocket and feeling, I must confess, a little swollen with success, I was greeted with open arms, with the same eagerness and affection that had awaited me at the end of every school year. This time I had a fresh sense of pride. On the road from the station to our concession there had been the most enthusiastic demonstrations of welcome, and they had all sprung from the same love and friendship. But while my parents embraced me—my mother was probably rejoicing more over my return than over the diploma—my mind was uneasy, especially so far as she was concerned.

Before I had left Conakry the director of the school had sent for me and asked me if I would like to go to France to finish my studies. I had blithely answered yes, but I had said it without having consulted my parents, without having consulted my mother. My uncles in Conakry had told me that it was a unique opportunity and that I didn't deserve to live if I turned it down. What would my parents say? Especially my mother? I did not feel at all comfortable. I waited until the first ecstatic greetings were over and then announced loudly, as if the news would be a source of delight to everyone:

"And that's not all: the director wants to send me to France!"

"To France?" my mother said.

I saw her face stiffen.

"Yes. I'm to be given a scholarship. It won't cost us anything."

"As if the cost mattered! So you're going to leave us again."

"Well, I'm not sure."

I could see that what I had been afraid of had happened. I had been too hasty in saying yes to the director.

"You're not going!" she said.

"No. But it wouldn't be for more than a year."

"A year?" said my father. "A year? That's not so very long."

"What?" my mother broke in sharply. "A year isn't so very long? For the last four years our son has been with us only on holidays, and you stand there and say a year is not so very long?"

"Well . . ." my father began.

"No, no! He's not going. That's that!"

"All right," my father said. "We won't speak of it again. This is the day of his return, his day of success. Let us rejoice. We'll talk about the other matter latter."

We said no more, for people were beginning to crowd into the concession, eager to celebrate my arrival.

Late that night when everyone was in bed I went and sat beside my father under the veranda of his hut. The director had told me he had to have my father's formal consent before he could do anything, and that it should reach him with as little delay as possible.

"Father," I said, "when the director asked me if I would like to go to France I said yes."

"Ah! You've already accepted."

"I couldn't help saying yes. I didn't think what I was saying at the time, or what you and my mother would think."

"Do you really want to go?"

"Yes. Uncle Mamadou says it's a unique opportunity."

"You could have gone to Dakar. Your uncle went to Dakar."

"It wouldn't be the same thing."

"No, it wouldn't. But how are we going to break the news to your mother?"

"Then you agree I should go?"

"Yes. . . . Yes, I'm willing. For your sake. For your own good."

And he was silent a while.

"It's something I've often thought about," he said. "I've thought about it night and day. I knew quite well that eventually you would leave us. I knew it the very first time you set foot in school. I watched you studying with such eagerness, such passionate eagerness! . . . Yes, since that day I have known how it would be. And gradually I resigned myself to it."

"Father!"

"Each one follows his own destiny, my son. Men can not change what is decreed. Your uncles too have had an education. As for me—but I've already told you; remember what I said when you went away to Conakry—I hadn't the opportunities they had, let alone yours. This opportunity is within your reach. You must seize it. You've already seized one, seize this one too, make sure of it. There are still so many things to be done in our land. . . . Yes, I want you to go to France. I want that now, just as much as you do. Soon we'll be needing men like you here. . . . May you not be gone too long!"

We sat under the veranda for a long time without saying anything, looking out into the night. Then suddenly my father said in a broken voice:

"Promise me that you will come back."

"I will come back."

"Those distant lands . . ." he whispered slowly.

He left the phrase unfinished and continued to stare into the darkness. I could see him by the light of the storm lantern, staring as if at a fixed point and frowning as if he were dissatisfied at what he saw.

"What are you looking at?" I asked.

"Take care never to deceive anyone," he said. "Be upright in thought and deed. And God will be with you."

Then he made what seemed a gesture of despair and turned his eyes away from the darkness.

The next day I wrote the director that my father had given

his permission. I kept it a secret from everyone but Kouyaté. Then I began a tour of the district. I had been given a pass and took the train wherever I wanted. I visited the nearby towns. I went to Kankan, our holy city. When I returned my father showed me the letter the director had sent him. It confirmed my departure and named the French school where I was to study. It was at Argenteuil.

"Do you know where Argenteuil is?" he asked.

"No. I'll go and have a look."

I looked it up in my dictionary and saw that it was only a few miles from Paris.

"It's near Paris," I said.

And I began to dream about Paris. I had heard about Paris for so long! Then my thoughts returned abruptly to my mother.

"Have you told her yet?" I asked.

"No. We'll go together."

"You wouldn't like to tell her yourself?"

"By myself? No, my son. Believe me, even if we both go we'll be outnumbered."

We went to look for her. We found her crushing millet for the evening meal. My father stood watching the pestle falling in the mortar. He scarcely knew where to begin. The decision he had had to make would hurt my mother, and his own heart was heavy. He stood there watching the pestle and saying nothing. I dared not lift my eyes. But she was not long in guessing what was up. She had only to look at us to understand everything or almost everything.

"What do you want?" she asked. "Can't you see I'm busy?"

And she began pounding faster and faster.

"Don't go so fast," my father said. "You'll wear yourself out."

"Are you teaching me how to pound millet?" she asked.

Then all of a sudden she went on angrily: "If it's about the boy's going to France you can save your breath. He's not going!"

"That's just it," said my father. "You don't know what you're talking about. You don't realize what such an opportunity means to him."

"I don't want to know."

Suddenly she dropped the pestle and took a few steps toward us.

"Am I never to have peace? Yesterday it was the school in Conakry; today it's the school in France; tomorrow . . . what will it be tomorrow? Every day there's some mad scheme to take my son away from me! . . . Have you already forgotten how sick he was in Conakry? But that's not enough for you. Now you want to send him to France! Are you crazy? Or do you want to drive me out of my mind? I'll certainly end up raving mad. . . . And as for you," she cried, turning to me, "you are nothing but an ungrateful son. Any excuse is good enough for you to run away from your mother. But this time it won't be as *you* want. You'll stay right here. Your place is here. . . . What *are* they thinking about at the school? Do they imagine I'm going to live my whole life apart from my son? Die with him far away? Have they no mothers, those people? They can't have. They wouldn't have gone so far away from home if they had."

She lifted up her eyes to the sky and addressed the heavens:

"He's been away from me so many years already! And now they want to take him away to their own land! . . ."

Then she lowered her gaze and looked at my father again: "Would you let them do that? Have you no heart?"

"Woman! Woman! Don't you know it's for his own good?"

"His own good? The best thing for him is to stay here with us. Hasn't he learned enough already?"

"Mother," I began.

But she turned on me violently:

"You be quiet! You're still just a little boy, a nobody. What do you want to go so far away for? Do you have any idea how people live out there? . . . No, you don't know anything about it. And tell me this, who's going to look after you? Who's going to mend your clothes? Who'll cook for you?"

"Come, come," said my father. "Be reasonable. The white men don't die of hunger."

"So you haven't noticed, you poor crazy thing, you haven't even noticed that they don't eat the way we do. The child will fall sick; that's what will happen. And then what will I do? What will become of me? Oh! I had a son once, but now I have none!"

I went up to her and took her in my arms.

"Get away from me!" she shouted. "You're no son of mine!"

But she did not push me away. She was weeping and she held me close.

"You won't leave me alone, will you? Tell me you won't leave me all alone."

But now she knew that I would go away and that she could not stop me, that nothing could stop me. Perhaps she had

known from the first. Yes, she must have guessed that this was
a matter where there were wheels within wheels. They had
taken me from the school in Kouroussa to Conakry and
finally to France. All the time she had been talking and fight-
ing against them she must have been watching the wheels
going round and round: first this wheel, then that, and then
a third and greater wheel, then still more, many more, perhaps, which no one could see. And how could they be stopped?
We could only watch them turning and turning, the wheels
of destiny turning and turning. My destiny was to go away
from home. And my mother began to turn her anger on those
who, she thought, were taking me away from her. But by now
her anger was futile: "Those people are never satisfied. They
want to have everything. As soon as they set eyes on something they want it for themselves."

"You shouldn't malign them," I replied.

"No," she said bitterly. "I shall not malign them."

Finally her anger and her rage were spent. She laid her
head on my shoulder and wept loudly. My father had crept
away. I held her close, I dried her tears, I said . . . what did
I say to her? Everything and anything that came into my head
but nothing of any importance. I don't think she understood
a word. All she was aware of was the sound of my voice.
That was enough. Her sobs gradually became quieter and
less frequent. . . .

That was how my departure was arranged. And so one day
I took a plane for France. Oh! it was a terrible parting! I do
not like to think of it. I can still hear my mother wailing.
I can still see my father, unable to hide his tears. I can still

see my sisters, my brothers. . . . No, I do not like to remember that parting. It was as if I were being torn apart.

In Conakry the director told me that the plane would land at Orly.

"From Orly," he said, "you will be taken to Paris, to the Gare des Invalides. There you will take the *métro* to the Gare Saint-Lazare, and then the train to Argenteuil."

He unfolded a map of the Paris *métro* and showed me my route underground. But the map meant nothing to me. The very idea of the *métro* was extremely vague.

"Are you sure you understand?"

"Yes."

But I did not quite understand everything.

"Take the map with you."

I slipped it into my pocket. He looked at me.

"You're not overdressed."

I was wearing white cotton trousers, a sleeveless sports shirt open at the throat, sandals, and white socks.

"You'll have to dress warmer over there. This time of year it's already beginning to get colder."

I left for the airport with Marie and my uncles. Marie was going with me as far as Dakar where she was to continue her education. Marie. . . . I got into the plane with her. I was crying. We were all crying. Then the propeller began to turn. In the distance my uncles were waving to us for the last time. The earth, the land of Guinea, began to drop rapidly away. . . .

"Are you glad to be going?" Marie asked me when the plane was nearing Dakar.

"I don't know. I don't think so."

And when we landed she asked me: "Will you be coming back?"

Her face was wet with tears.

"Yes," I said. "Yes . . ."

I nodded yes again as I fell back in my seat, for I did not want anyone to see my tears. Surely I would be coming back! I sat a long while without moving, my arms tightly folded to stifle the sobs that wracked me. . . .

Later on I felt something hard when I put my hand in my pocket. It was the map of the *métro*. . . .